"Scott's insights to the true identity of the Fruit of the Spirit are well beyond his years, and a testament to his gifting as a teacher in the Body of Christ."

Rev. Dr. Ray Vinson, LFT., Th.D, Ph.D

BEARING MUCH FRUIT

Growing Spiritual Fruit for Everyday Living

Scott W Rasco

Bearing Much Fruit

©2018 Scott W Rasco

All rights reserved. No portion of this book may be reproduced, stored in a retrieval system, or transmitted in any form or by any means--electronic, mechanical, photocopy, recording, scanning, or other--except for brief quotations in critical reviews or articles, without the prior written permission of the publisher.

For more information contact:

    GRAPH Publishing, LLC.

    www.graphpublishing.com

Printed and Bound by:

    Ingram Publisher Services

Bible quotations are given in KJV unless otherwise noted:

The Holy Bible: King James Version. electronic ed. of the 1769 edition of the 1611 Authorized Version. Bellingham WA: Logos Research Systems, Inc., 1995.

2018 Cover Art Designed by Scott Rasco

To Jen,

Thanks for supporting my work and being my editor and proofreader. I know sometimes it seems overwhelming, but you have always stood with me. Words cannot express what I feel. You are the greatest soul mate anyone could ask for. I love you.

TABLE OF CONTENTS

About the Author — ix

Part 1 Learning to Truly Live

Chapter 1 – Beginning the Spiritual Life	- 15 -
Chapter 2 – The Basics of Growing Fruit	- 24 -
Chapter 3 – Begin Preparing the Soil	- 32 -
Chapter 4 – Renewing Nutrients	- 38 -
Chapter 5 – Plant the Seed	- 49 -

Part 2 Spiritual Cultivation

Chapter 6 – Maintain Growth	- 59 -
Chapter 7 – Pruning Away Decay	- 68 -
Chapter 8 – Purging the Chaff	- 78 -
Chapter 9 – Harvest Time	- 86 -

Part 3 The Nature of the Spirit

Chapter 10 – Spirit Versus the Flesh	- 95 -
Chapter 11 – Gifts of Grace	- 102 -

Part 4 The Fruit of the Spirit

Chapter 12 – The Fruit of Love	- 117 -
Chapter 13 – The Fruit of Joy	- 126 -
Chapter 14 – The Fruit of Peace	- 136 -
Chapter 15 – The Fruit of Patience	- 147 -
Chapter 16 – The Fruit of Gentleness	- 154 -
Chapter 17 – The Fruit of Goodness	- 162 -
Chapter 18 – The Fruit of Faithfulness	- 169 -
Chapter 19 – The Fruit of Meekness	- 183 -
Chapter 20 – The Fruit of Self-Control	- 187 -

Part 5 Applying the Principles to Life

Chapter 21 – All Wrapped up in Love	- 197 -
Chapter 22 – Corporate Fruit Bearing	- 203 -
Chapter 23 – No Fruit?	- 213 -
Chapter 24 – Empowered to Shine	- 218 -

Works Cited	- 227 -

About the Author

As a child, I felt the call of God overshadowing my life. I always wanted to know and understand the Love of God and truly grasp his presence. I grew up in a "Christian" home and was raised in a Spirit Filled Church.

Even though, I was saved at the age of 5, I remained confused about my relationship with God and his true love and grace. At the Age of 13, I fell into a deep, dark depression. In the midst of depression, I learned the greatest warfare that I possessed: Worship.

I would spend hours just singing my heart out to God. I would write and read the Bible. My heart was always to teach others. God gave me the vision to reach the hurting through music and God's Word. I have never been satisfied seeing people saved, but rather to see hearts set free.

I began ministering in worship, drama, and media arts at the age of 15, then moved into youth leadership when I started college. During high school and college, I also began writing short stories, music, and dramatic productions.

I had the privilege of marrying the love of my life in 2002 and after a devastating miscarriage in 2004, we had our oldest boys in 2005 and 2006. God blessed us with another bundle of joy in 2010 when we were asked to care for and ultimately adopt our daughter. Then in 2013 we began the road of foster care for our daughter's biological brother who suffers from high functioning autism spectrum disorder. Since then we have cared for over 40 children in our home and are strong advocates for foster and adoptive parenting as well as the rights of special needs children.

I received my Bachelor of Science degree in Religion from Liberty University in 2004 and was ordained as a minister in the state of Texas in 2005 following my move into preaching and evangelism. I then finished my Master of Divinity degree from Logsdon Seminary in 2007.

God has opened many doors to minister at different levels of Pastoral ministry, but I feel the mandate of my call is to demonstrate the love of God to the hurting world. The greatest way to reach the lost is through the redemptive power of Jesus Christ. God is in the business of bringing healing and deliverance. Even in the church there are many people who suffer from the bondage of fear. With the plethora of stressors in our lives no one is immune to dread and anxiety. Paul instructs us in 2 Timothy 1:7, "God has not given us a spirit of fear, but of power and love and of a sound mind."

It does not matter what the world tells us, we were bought with a price and we do not have to blindly accept the lies of the enemy. Instead, it is time that we take back what the devil has stolen: our peace.

For booking appearances and ministry information

Contact us at cultivatespirit@rocketmail.com

Or you can contact Graph Publishing, LLC at graphpublishingllc@gmail.com

PART 1
LEARNING TO TRULY LIVE

It is not death that a man should fear,
but he should fear never beginning to live.

--Marcus Aurelius[1]

---

[1] Aurelius, Marcus, *Meditations*, (Brooklyn, NY: Sheba Blake Publishing. 2015), p. 144.

Chapter 1 – Beginning the Spiritual Life

What is the real value of life? Is it simply a journey that we travel, and upon the end of that journey we will no longer exist? Is it a path that we will follow, and upon death we return to move into another life somewhere else? Or do we adhere to the idea that upon death there is a place where we will dwell for all of eternity?

Most of the world religions have some concept of life after death. Many, like Buddhism and Hinduism, believe in a time of reincarnation until enlightenment. Some other religions believe in a realm of the dead. The Old Testament Jewish idea of Sheol was much like the Greek idea of the underworld. It was a place where the Spirit dwelled when a person died.[2] Still other religions believe that the human soul exists for eternity and will live forever somewhere.

No matter what we believe, most religions believe in spirituality. Spirituality is the condition of being spiritual. Basically, it is the concept of being more than simply physical. There is more to life than just breathing. Islam calls this the Greater Jihad, which is the attempt to live a righteous or upright life.

---

[2] Heiser, Michael S, "Old Testament Theology of the Afterlife," In *Faithlife Study Bible*, (Bellingham, WA: Lexham Press, 2016).

Many Christians believe that we live life working to overcome sin. Such disciples strive to live a proper life doing the best they can and hope it is good enough. However, Jesus came to the earth so that we could have life and have it in abundance. He came to empower us to overcome the actions of sin and to obtain the spiritual nature.

There is much more to this life than just preparing to die. Instead, God created every one of us to live. He created us to thrive in this present life, not just in the life to come. When Jesus said that he came to give life abundantly, that meant a life that overflows into others. It is a life that extends the kingdom of God from just you or me, to the people we encounter.

Who is this book for?

The purpose of this book is to help people discover the importance of the spiritual life and understand how to incorporate the fruit of the Spirit into daily living. Furthermore, it is to assist believers in gaining a deeper understanding of the relationship and comparison between the human nature and the spiritual nature.

This book was created for people of all different levels of spirituality. Part One is geared toward new believers who have begun their walk with Christ but need some extra support. When we first begin following Jesus, there are many things that we learn as we develop a deeper relationship with Him. Part One lays the groundwork for the remainder of the book.

Veteran Christians may already know most of this preliminary information, but it can be good for us to be reminded, and it may provide new understanding as we look at the comparison between bearing natural fruit and bearing spiritual fruit. The Parts Two and Three of the book deal deeper with practical application of spirituality, while Part Four offers a deeper understanding of each of the fruits of the Spirit. Finally, Part Five examines several specific issues with spiritual fruit bearing.

What does it mean to live a spiritual life?

Humanity is rooted in the flesh, which is also called carnality. This body seeks to satisfy itself. It wants to satisfy its lusts and its desires. This is the carnal nature, and it comes from being human. As a human we can lust after anything. Though most people think of lust in a sexual connotation, lust is basically any form of overwhelming desire. The English word "lust" began as neutral term referring to any type of strong overwhelming desire.[3] That could include materialism, gluttony, infidelity and fornication, alcoholism, etc., in short, any type of overpowering desire.

In the beginning God creating human beings in perfection without sin. Nevertheless, when sin entered the world, the carnal nature of humanity began seeking after its own lusts instead of the perfection of God. Paul says Romans 7:18, "For I know in my flesh dwells nothing good." Since the carnal nature is the root of humanity, natural human nature is not inherently

---

[3] Tongue, D. H. "Lust." Edited by D. R. W. Wood, I. H. Marshall, A. R. Millard, J. I. Packer, and D. J. Wiseman, *New Bible Dictionary*. (Downers Grove, IL: InterVarsity Press, 1996).

good. It has no virtue in its own. The Psalmist said, "I was formed in iniquity, in sin did my mother conceive me."[4]

In the beginning there was no sin in the world. God did not create sin. Instead sin came from the rejection of God. Many of the angels fell because they rejected God. When they were created, Adam and Eve were sinless and innocent. As soon as they let the enemy deceive them, sin entered the world. As the children of Adam, sin dwells in us through nature. There is no way that we can get away from sin. Sin reigns in our lives. It is deeply rooted into the makeup of our flesh.

Since we were borne of the flesh, we are sinful in our basic human nature. We have nothing good within ourselves. Inherently we have no value to God. But God thought otherwise. We were created in His image. He loved us so much that He sent his only begotten Son and if we believe in Him, we will not perish but have eternal life.

Think of a hundred-dollar bill. Essentially, a hundred-dollar bill is not worth the linen paper that it was printed on. We no longer really have a system of finance based on precious metals. A hundred-dollar bill in the middle of the Amazon might be used for nothing more than bathroom tissue. The value of a hundred dollars is not based on the material that it is made from; rather it is based on the value we give it.

In the same way, we do not have a pure value on our own, but God thought us valuable enough that He gave His only Son for us. What greater love is there than a man who lays down his life for others? Many would easily lay down their lives for their families, but few would lay down their

---

[4] Psalms 51:5

lives for strangers. Nevertheless, Christ laid down his life for people who did not know Him. He went to His death not only for his disciples but those who were putting him to death. He paid the ultimate sacrifice for strangers who would come hundreds and even thousands of years later.

In a similar way the United States military goes to the ends of the earth to fight for the rights and freedom of others. Soldiers are willing to risk their lives for millions they do not know. They choose to fight to protect our liberty. Likewise, spiritual living is based on the sacrifice that the Lord Jesus made, and through His life, death, and resurrection, He enables us to have spiritual liberty.

How did He help us?

Have you ever noticed that almost every major religious group focuses on spiritual advancement through personal self-sacrifice? The Buddhists' way to enlightenment is to remove all desire so they then can have fulfilled lives. There are sects of Muslims that believe that the greatest spiritual sacrifice is suicide while, at the same time, killing as many of their enemies as possible. We can see that in almost every other religion the focus of most devout followers is to sacrifice for their god. Paradoxically, Christianity is the only religion where God came and sacrificed Himself for humanity.

Jesus came into the earth robed in flesh. He was God encompassed in the fleshly nature of humankind. While most religions focus on the need to overcome sin and the desires of the flesh, Jesus also taught a gospel of mercy and grace. The first step to true repentance is accepting the mercy of God and admitting that in ourselves we are not capable of living a holy life.

Beginning the Spiritual Life

Once we discover that we are powerless, and that He is all powerful, we can then allow Him to enter in, and through His Spirit we are empowered to overcome the enemy.

I believe that it was only through God coming to earth that He could truly understand what it was like to be human. God's only way of truly knowing what it was like to be human was to enter the flesh Himself.

When I was in high school, I had the opportunity to read a book called *Chosen to Live* by David Kelton. It was one of the first books I ever chose to read on my own without being forced by a teacher to do so. It is an autobiographical sketch of a man who spent many years chasing after the life of the flesh and the sins thereof. In the story, he finally accepts the saving work of Jesus Christ. Kelton tells of an experience he had, post-conversion, when he tried to save a dog that was fearfully stranded in the middle of the road. Cars were dodging the poor animal, but the freezing weather made this an even more dangerous situation.

Kelton stopped his car and trudged across the road to save the dog, but every time he got close the dog would run. Finally, for his own safety Kelton had to give up. Upon Kelton getting back in his car, he felt God speak to his heart. God said, "That is how I felt with you all of those years. I tried to catch you and save you. The more I tried to save you, the more you ran."[5]

In much the same way, God chased after lost humanity throughout the Old Testament, but people never really understood Him. They just continued to run after the lust of the flesh. It took God coming to the earth

---

[5] Kelton, David, *Chosen To live*, (New Kensington, PA: Whitaker House, 1986), p.145.

as a human for Him to truly be able to communicate with us in a way that we could understand.

In Hebrews 2 starting with verse 16, it says that Jesus took on the nature of the children of Abraham. It explains, "It behooved Him to be like unto His brothers that He might be a merciful and faithful high priest…" "Behooved" is not a common, twenty-first century word. It means obligation of necessity, as does its Greek counterpart from which it was translated. Jesus' coming to earth was necessary for Him to be able to be a faithful and merciful high priest.

The New Testament high priests did not serve out of love and compassion; rather they served out of duty. It was simply a job. They had become arrogant and merciless, quick to judge and without pity. (I know Christians like this.) The priests acted out of arrogance and had no connection with the people. This caused them to forget what it was like to be lost.

On the contrary, Jesus was a faithful and merciful high priest, He was able to show love and compassion to reach the lost[6]. He lived as a human and understood what it was like to be flesh. Verse 18 says that because He was tempted, He can bring aid to those who are tempted.

In the Gospels we find accounts of Jesus being tempted by the devil. But those were not the only times that Jesus was tempted. The writer of Hebrews in chapter 4, verse 15, said that Jesus was tempted in all ways that humanity is tempted. The difference is that we have sinned, and He

---

[6] Wuest, Kenneth S, *Wuest's Word Studies from the Greek New Testament : For the English Reader*, (Grand Rapids: Eerdmans, 1997), p.48.

was tempted but did not sin. Nevertheless, He, who never sinned, was made sin for us so that we could become the righteousness of God.[7] We have the power over sin through the sacrifice of Jesus Christ. God did not ask us to suffer for Him; He suffered so that we could have life.

Why must the seed die?

Something must happen before a seed can bear fruit; it must die. Jesus said to his disciples in John 12:24, "Except a corn of wheat fall into the ground and die, it abides alone, but if it dies, it brings forth much fruit." If a seed is left by itself, it is nothing more than a seed. However, when that seed is planted and allowed to take root, life begins to spring forth, and it can produce much more fruit.

The story is told about a man who was walking through the desert. He was parched and thirsty, and there was no end in sight. He happened upon what seemed to be a small dwelling with an old water pump. He ran to the pump and started pumping, but no water emerged from its mouth. The man, disheartened, noticed a small container of water with a note that said, "Use this to prime the pump." He had a very big choice to make, did he use the water in the jar to prime the pump and have an endless supply of water, or did he drink it and satisfy his immediate thirst? If he primed the pump but it did not work, then he would lose the only water he had. On the other hand, if he drank it, he would quickly become thirsty again.

After weighing the options, he slowly primed the pump. He raised the pump arm, but nothing happened. He again raised the pump arm, and

---

[7] 1 Corinthians 5:21

nothing happened. By the third time he was ready to give up. He raised the pump arm, expecting nothing to happen, when suddenly water began gushing out of the mouth of the pump. He lapped up the water, let it run all over his face, and filled up every container that he could find. When he had a chance to rest and was about to go, he turned over the note. It said, "Please refill the vessel to help someone else." Just like the pump had to be primed before the water would come out, if we do not plant the seed, then the seed cannot produce.

Looking back at the verse from John 12, Jesus' reference to the death of the seed alluded to His own death. Without His death we would not have the opportunity for life. He took on our sin so that He could pay the price that we owed. As slaves to sin, we all were on the road to death and hell. Romans 6:23 reveals to us that the wage of sin is death. Jesus paid our debt so that we could be free.

As we referred to earlier, He came so that we could have life in abundance. Through His saving grace we are free from the laws of sin and of death. But we must allow that the spiritual seed to grow inside of us. It is time for us to move past the nature of our humanity so that we can live through the power of Jesus Christ. In this text, we will be looking at the cultivation of the Spirit and allowing the Spirit of God to change our lives.

Chapter 2 – The Basics of Growing Fruit

Have you ever planted a garden? Planting a garden begins with tilling the ground before we can plant the seed. Then we must maintain the growth of the plants through proper maintenance before we can see a harvest. It takes a lot of hard work and dedication. If it were not for the people who love farming, there would be no fresh produce for us to buy in the store. The people who lived many thousands of years ago, during the era of the hunters and gatherers, did very little gardening. Mostly they ate roots and plants that grew around and hunted wild game to eat. While they moved around following the migrating herds of animals, individuals had little time to wait for the harvest time to come. As people began forming civilizations, settling the land, and making permanent/semi-permanent residences, farming became a part of life.

Today, farming remains vital to our existence. It not only provides the food on our tables, it also supplies work for many Americans. It is a very important industry. On a smaller scale millions of people every year have backyard gardens: vegetable gardens, flower gardens, rose gardens, and rock gardens though I think it would be very hard to grow a rock.

I am personally not a gardener in the physical realm, but rather a gardener of the soul. In this chapter, we will relate the process of planting and harvesting to spiritual growth. Just as the earth is prepared, and steps are taken to properly maintain growth, in our spiritual life we also need to be actively involved in our spiritual formation and development.

What kind of fruit are we growing?

To begin our spiritual development, we need to first understand what we are growing. When we plant an apple tree, we do not get bananas, and when we plant a corn seed, we do not get a tomato plant. A few years ago, there was a wonderful coming-of-age movie called *Secondhand Lions*. It was about two elderly, wealthy brothers who helped to raise their young nephew.

They were very frugal and felt that anyone who came to visit was after their money. One day a man came to sell them some vegetable seeds. Putting their reluctance aside, they decided to buy some seeds and plant a garden. Everything was great, until the day they noticed that all the shoots that were growing looked exactly alike. The salesman had conned them into buying packages of the same seed with different labels.

In Paul's writing to the church at Galatia he said, "Be not deceived; God is not mocked: for whatsoever a man soweth, that shall he also reap. For he that soweth to his flesh shall of the flesh reap corruption; but he that soweth to the Spirit shall of the Spirit reap life everlasting."[8] This passage can be a little difficult to understand at first glance, so we can unpack it a little to better comprehend what the author was trying to tell us.

---

[8] Galatians 6:7-8

The Basics of Growing Fruit

In the NCV[9] translation It says, "Do not be fooled: You cannot cheat God. People harvest only what they plant." I like this version of the passage because it shines more light on the first two phases of the verse.

In the first two phases, Paul points out a common misconception that we tend to accept. Far too many people live a life of deceit and believe they will receive from it a life of blessing. They seek things out of selfish, vain pursuit, then fool themselves, and even others, into believing that good things will come of it. Paul reminds us of the natural and spiritual law of sowing and reaping. We will reap what we plant.

In the same way, if we plant a potato, we will not grow cabbage, and if we plant selfishness, we will only gain things of the flesh. On the other hand, if we plant things of the Spirit we will develop, or harvest, the fruit of the Spirit. For instance, if we plant dissension, we will harvest anger and confusion. If we plant trust, we will grow love and compassion.

Most Christians would immediately equate the word corruption, from the third phrase, to Hell or eternal damnation. That is a simple assumption because Paul has just said those who sow to the Spirit will reap everlasting life

But if Paul intended people to make that connection, why did he use the word corruption? Corruption signifies destruction, moral decay, and perishing[10]. Essentially, it refers to things which can perish or be corrupted. In Matthew 6:19-20, Jesus tells us not store up for ourselves treasures on

---

[9] New Century Version

[10] Strong, James, *The Exhaustive Concordance of the Bible : Showing Every Word of the Text of the Common English Version of the Canonical Books, and Every Occurrence of Each Word in Regular Order*, electronic ed, (Ontario: Woodside Bible Fellowship, 1996), G5356.

earth where moth and rust can corrupt. Basically, in these two passages the word "corrupt" refers to something that is temporary, easily destroyed, or perishable.

Some people work on their bodies all the time to have the perfect physique, but when they die, what good was it? Think of the number of weight lifters who did everything they could to become the best and destroyed their health and bodies due to steroid and drug abuse. Athletes many times destroy their physical bodies to play a sport or compete in an event. Though the glory of what they achieve is great, the damage of what it took for that achievement is life altering.

Understandably, health is important, but a person must balance that cost of what he or she is trying to achieve. When we sow into this dying physical body, we will ultimately still reap death. No matter how much money actors and actresses spend on "nips and tucks," they are truly just prolonging the inevitable. Furthermore, they will be putting into the ground a very expensive corpse.

I often tell this joke when I am preaching. A 70-year-old woman had an accident and while unconscious she went to heaven. There she saw God. She asked, "Am I dead?"

God answered, "No, you have twenty-five more years ahead of you." Within just a few minutes she regained consciousness, and, after spending the night in the hospital, she was released to go home. She immediately went to a plastic surgeon. She told the surgeon that she was going to live for twenty-five more years, so she wanted the body of a thirty-year-old.

Within a week she had been tucked everywhere that could be tucked and stretched everywhere that could be stretched. After many weeks of recovery, she finally had the body of a thirty-year-old. She stepped out of the hospital door and was hit by an ambulance. Upon returning to heaven she was irate. She looked at God and said, "You said I had twenty-five more years. What happened?"

God looked closer and said, "Oh, I am so sorry, I did not recognize you."

Obviously, that story is not real, but that sentiment is. The things of the world will someday fade away. No matter what we do, this body will someday die. No matter how much money a person earns, it is no good in the grand scheme of eternity. No matter how many friends a person has, someday they will all be gone. That is what Paul means by "corruption". The things we do for Christ are all that matters in the end.

The purpose of this book is to delve deeper into the understanding of bearing spiritual fruit. In the fourth phase of the verse, Paul stated that a person who sows to the Spirit will harvest eternal life. Another way to understand this is reaping things that matter spiritually. While things of the flesh will decay and perish, things we reap of Spirit will last for eternity. For this reason, in Galatians 5:22, Paul tells us of nine characteristics of spiritual living. He calls them the fruit of the Spirit. They are "love, joy, peace, patience, gentleness, goodness, faith, meekness, [and] self-control." These characteristics go above and beyond normal self-serving acts and are produced by the work of the Spirit of God inside of us.

How do we define spiritual fruit?

A fruit is typically defined as produce. Not only is it produced by a plant, but in most cases, it houses the basic structure for producing another plant. Have you ever seen an old peach tree growing in a location where few people tend to go? Its fruit lies on the ground until the flesh has decayed and all that is left is the seed. Then within a year or so little sprouts begin to burst through the ground where the seeds had fallen.

Fruit is amazing. It grows from different plants such as trees, bushes, and vines. It begins as a bud that quickly turns into a flower. Within a few weeks that bud develops into mature fruit that can be harvested and eaten. The flowering stage is one of the most eye-catching parts of the fruit growing process, but it is also one of the shortest. Most of the fruiting process is done with little to no outward demonstration. In the same way, most Christian growth is done with little to no outward evidence. In many cases, growth is so subtle that outsiders do not notice it at first.

Jesus said in Matthew 7:16, "You will know them by their fruit." In no way are we supposed to live our lives so that the world can notice our works, but when we allow the Spirit to change us, people notice. When an alcoholic gets saved and begins to live a Christian life, his friends notice a difference. When the Spirit changes a human heart, family and friends notice the change. They may not know why, but they notice that something is different.

When the flower falls, the bud grows, and the small fruit begins to mature. In the same way, when we are in the flowering stage, we may not be producing fruit, but the world knows there is something different. As time goes by, and the more we grow, we begin to bear fruit. It may seem like a very slow process, and slowly but surely, we grow.

As was just mentioned, the fruit typically contains the seed. When a seed is planted, it can turn into a plant or tree which grows more fruit. Spiritually, this happens in two different ways. When the Spirit develops fruit in us, one fruit will lead to another. For instance, as we develop kindness, patience will grow, and as we develop faith, peace begins to grow. Each of the fruits of the Spirit works simultaneously to develop different areas of our lives.

Furthermore, as the Spirit works in us, it can also help to bear fruit in other people. The more love we show to someone else, the more we assist the love growing in them. What we do for others will be reciprocated. We also help promote growth in each other. As I grow stronger, I can help someone else grow stronger, and that person can then help me in my weakness. It is a cycle. The more we demonstrate the fruits of the Spirit, the more we should notice similar fruits showing up in the lives of others.

Moreover, a literal fruit does not spring forth from the stem of a plant or the stalk itself; instead it grows from the branch. Picture a pecan tree. We never see pecans growing straight out of the trunk of a tree. Instead, the trunk separates into smaller branches, and the pecans are produced on those branches. Even on a grape vine, the fruit does not come directly off the stalk, but from small branches that sprout out from it.

Jesus said, "Abide in me, and I in you. As the branch cannot bear fruit of itself, except it abide in the vine; no more can ye, except ye abide in me. I am the vine, ye *are* the branches: He that abideth in me, and I in him, the same bringeth forth much fruit; for without me ye can do nothing."

The vine is the life-source for the branch. This allows the branch to bring forth the fruit. Without the vine the branch dies. In the same way, God is the life source that enables us to bear fruit which is utilized in our daily walk. As we allow God to use us, the more the Spirit can bear these fruits in our lives, and the more we can be involved in the Kingdom of God.

Chapter 3 – Begin Preparing the Soil

Preparing the soil is the first thing we must do when we decide to plant a garden. There are so many different types of soil. In the part of Texas where I live we have a lot of farmers. When I was about eight years old, we began spending Sundays at a cousin's house, and I had the chance to explore most of their land. I remember looking over the fence and seeing the beautiful coffee-colored soil that had freshly been tilled and ready for planting. I remember noticing another field where the soil was red and dusty. I discovered that it made up mostly of sand and was suitable for growing peanuts.

The differences of the soil in natural gardening is very similar to the differences in spiritual cultivation. There are many different levels of spirituality and spiritual growth. Since people are different and at diverse places on their spiritual walk, there is no one-size-fits-all solution. All soils are different, and some can support growth while others cannot.

In much the same way all peoples' hearts are different. Before a person can grow spiritually, the individual must allow God to prepare the his or her heart. Jesus explains this in the *Parable of the Sower*, Matthew 13:3-8:

Behold, a sower went forth to sow; ⁴ And when he sowed, some *seeds* fell by the wayside and the fowls came and devoured them up: ⁵ Some fell upon stony places, where they had not much earth: and forthwith they sprung up, because they had no deepness of earth: ⁶ And when the sun was up, they were scorched; and because they had no root, they withered away. ⁷ And some fell among thorns; and the thorns sprung up, and choked them: ⁸ But others fell into good ground, and brought forth fruit, some a hundredfold, some sixtyfold, some thirtyfold.

In this passage the sower is God, and the seed is His Word. Additionally**,** the soil is the hearts of those who hear the Word. In the allegory, there are multiple locations where seed was sown. Some locations were conducive to growth; others were not. We will examine the specific locations in future sections. It is important to understand that even when we readily accept the Word of God in our lives, we can allow certain factors in to destroy the work of Christ in our hearts.

Why is the proper location important?

Every experienced farmer or gardener knows that to grow, plants need a location that is conducive for growth. To be conducive to growing, the plants' location needs three things: soil, water, and sunlight. If these three things are accessible, there is a high probability that the plants will take root and mature.

Initially, the type of soil in a garden plays one of the most important roles. Different soils have different characteristics. Some soils are made up of clay and are hard to work with. Other areas have a lot of sand and can only support certain types of plants. Selecting the right type of soil for the plants we are wanting to grow plays a big part in whether our efforts at gardening are successful.

Furthermore, the location must have proper water and drainage as well as adequate sunlight. Without these attributes our plants will not grow.

Similarly, our hearts also can have certain negative factors that impede spiritual growth. For instance, unforgiveness and hatred lead to aggression and anguish and will interfere with our ability to develop a deeper relationship with Christ. On the other hand, a heart that is open to the Spirit of God and willing to be changed can grow more effectively. But it still needs the proper support from God's Word and other Christians to avoid being easily manipulated.

While the growth is in this initial phase, spiritual care is very important. If a natural plant does not have adequate water, then it will begin showing signs of dying within just a few days. This is also true in spiritual growth. If the spiritual thirst of a new believer is not properly encouraged, either by a church or friends and family, he or she may quickly fall away.

I remember in my undergraduate years having been taught that the greatest way to maintain new converts is by connecting the person with the church. This is done through friendship, volunteer opportunities, etc. Basically, if a person can get plugged in, or rooted, in a church, he or she is more likely to remain at the given church. Strategically speaking, where the person is planted will affect how he or she grows.

Nevertheless, different plants need different amounts of water, so we must take into account the type of plant that we are hoping to grow. If we are not careful, we can neglect a plant and not provide enough water. On the other hand, we can tend to the plant too much and end up drowning it.

I believe this to also be true in spiritual growth. For example, if a person becomes uncomfortable with overly spiritual services, loud music, and disco lights, he or she will probably not find the needed nurturing in a contemporary worship service in a charismatic church. On the other hand, a person who loves the club scene, concerts, and emotional connections might feel right at home. Different churches can meet the various needs of individuals and promote growth.

By the same token, a natural garden must have adequate light. A plant uses the carbohydrates from carbon dioxide and the hydrogen from water and releases oxygen. This process is aided by radiant light, especially the sun. Without some type of radiant light, plants cannot grow and develop.

Of course, the sun is the basic source of all energy on earth. The sun's energy begins the process of photosynthesis in plants. That energy is then carried from the plant into the animal that consumes the plant.

Natural plants seek out the sun. If we put a potted plant in a window, we will notice over time that the part of the plant closest to the sun's light will be more vibrant. Most plants will even begin growing toward the sun's light to ensure the greatest exposure. That is why my grandmother used to always turn potted plants from time to time to allow every part to receive adequate sun.

In the same way, God is the originator of our spiritual nature, and as we bear fruit, we pass on the light of God to other people. This will be discussed later, but for now we need to mention that the place we allow ourselves to be planted should nurture us with accurate Biblical teachings. In 2 Timothy 4:3b Paul says, "...after their own lusts shall they heap to themselves teachers, having itching ears." In other words, Paul explains that people tend to gravitate toward preachers and teachers who will tell them what they want to hear. But this is not conducive to spiritual growth. In order to grow spiritually, we should allow ourselves to be planted around others who are willing and able to challenge and inspire us to build a deeper relationship with God.

How does tilling help the ground?

After a farmer chooses the most appropriate location to sow his or her crops the farmer must then begin to till the ground. As Christians we, too, must begin "tilling the soil". As we mentioned earlier in this chapter, there are different characteristics about soil. Soil with a heavy clay content absorbs water slowly causing plants to be devoid of much needed hydration. Furthermore, tightly packed soil can also inhibit the transfer of water, leaving it to evaporate off the top soil before it can be absorbed.

In Jeremiah 4:3, it says, "Break up your fallow ground", referring to the heart. Jeremiah was talking to a group of hard-hearted Jews who were unreceptive to the Word of God. They had allowed themselves to be hardened by sin, rebellion, and lack of compassion for others. In Zechariah 7:12, the prophet says, "They have made their hearts as an adamant stone lest they should hear the law." The people's hearts were hardened toward God because they did not want to be subject to His law.

We see this even more in the New Testament when the Jews refused to acknowledge Jesus as the Christ. In John 1:11, it says, "He came unto his own, and his own received him not." Sadly, even today, people refuse to accept the loving work of the cross. They hear the Good News but refuse to allow the Word to penetrate their hearts.

Looking back at our passage about the sower, notice the ground where he was sowing. Some fell on good ground. That ground was ready for the seed. It readily accepted the seed and was filled with the proper nutrients for growth. The good, fertile soil produced a hundred, sixty, or thirty times what was originally sown. The soil had been prepared and made ready for the seed.

Just like a farmer tills the soil, we break up our hardened hearts through prayer and faithfulness to God. If we are hardened towards others, we must learn to show love and mercy. No matter the situation that caused the hardened heart, God can take away the pain and anguish and heal the brokenness. It is only when we are receptive that the seed of the Word takes root inside of our lives and begins to grow good fruit.

Nevertheless, preparing the location is just the first step in the process of spiritual growth.

Chapter 4 – Renewing Nutrients

In the last chapter we analyzed the necessity of preparing the soil. In a literal garden preparing the ground is vital for a strong healthy garden. Similarly, the farmer needs to maintain nutrients in the soil. Due to contaminates and extreme usage, much of today's soil is devoid of many of its natural nutrients. God saw this as a very big problem in the Bible. In Exodus 23:10, it says, "Six years thou shalt sow thy land…But the seventh year thou shalt let it rest and lie still."

In the beginning, God created the universe in six days. On the seventh day God rested. He instituted the tradition of the Sabbath. In the Torah, God constituted that there would be no work on the Sabbath. Even the Ten Commandments said, "Honor the Sabbath day and keep it holy." For this reason, the idea of the Sabbath was very prominent in the Jewish culture.

Nevertheless, in the New Testament Jesus attempts to correct the Jewish misconception of the purpose of the Sabbath. This is evident throughout the Gospels because Jesus converses with the Jewish leaders on multiple occasions regarding the true necessity of the Sabbath. In Mark 2:27, Jesus explains that the Sabbath was initiated for humankind not humankind created to honor the Sabbath. In other words, God provided the Sabbath so that humankind could take a much-needed rest. Sadly, many of the Jews in Jesus' day used the Sabbath as another way to put more restrictions on their people.

People need a rest or a break, so they are not over-worked and suffer burn out. Sadly, even though rest is vital for health and personal welfare, it has been said that the United States has the lowest rate of people taking time to rest.[11] Understandably, it also has the highest rate of burnout. People are working themselves to death because the human body cannot handle the constant strain that we put on it.

Correspondingly, the earth also needs rest to recuperate after the years of sowing and reaping. God told the Children of Israel that they could plant and reap for six years, but the seventh year the land had to be allowed to rest. Moreover, if a Jewish farmer owned Jewish slaves, the slaves would work for six years, and on the seventh year the slaves would be freed, and all debts would be forgiven.

Sadly, we read in the prophecies of Jeremiah that the people were no longer honoring the sabbatical year. In Jeremiah 25, the prophet warns the people that God was about to take them into captivity for seventy years. Then in Jeremiah 34, the prophet explains that seventy years of exile was a punishment for the people's refusal to offer freedom to their Jewish slaves every seventh year. Also, in 2 Chronicles 36:21, the Bible expounds that the

---

[11] Schelmetic, Tracey E. "Lack of Vacation Leads to Burnout and Loss of Productivity." *Workforce Management Today*. November 18, 2013. http://www.workforcemanagementtoday.com/articles/360683-lack-vacation-leads-burnout-lost-productivity.htm (accessed July 17, 2018).

seventy years of exile were to also repay the land for the generations of missed sabbatical rests.

Spiritually, we need rest as well. Psalms 46:10 reminds the believer to be still or not worry because God is going to take care of all things. He will take care of all the attacks of the enemy for the glory of God. Therefore, we can opt to rest in His promises instead of remaining fearful. As we rest in Him, we rejuvenate our hearts and minds, allowing us to grow and bear more fruit.

Use manure, really?

Growing up, I always thought that fertilizer was simply a food for plants; however, fertilizer is used to replace the missing nutrients in the soil brought on by continued usage. When preparing for a garden, in addition to allowing it to rest, it is very important that we renew the nutrients in the soil through the adding of fertilizers. Although there are many types of fertilizers, many farmers and gardeners will still utilize organic compounds such as compost and manure. As these fertilizers deteriorate, the much-needed nutrients for the soil are rejuvenated to feed the plants.

As anything breaks down due to decay, it stinks. Death and rot stink. If a gardener sets aside biological products and allows it to compost, the decay and rot cause a natural earthy stench as does the other main organic fertilizer, manure. As it breaks down, like compost, it provides the same nutrients.

I remember my second spring in college; I was attending a state university about forty-five miles from my home. The commute was on an old, winding road that went through two very small towns which had many dairy farms. I remember driving at five-thirty in the morning and being infiltrated with the smell of the manure. It was the worst thing I had ever smelled. I also hated when the dairy hands would get paid and come in to the restaurant where I worked. Every other Friday we would have truckloads of dairy workers come in to eat, and then we were left to clean the manure off the floor that was left by their covered work boots.

Though manure has one of the very worst smells, it is one of the strongest fertilizers and has been used for centuries. If a person can overlook the horrendous smell, the benefit of this natural plant food can yield some of the best produce. Similarly, God can use the "manure" of life to help produce the greatest harvest of spiritual fruit.

As I look back on my life, I realize that I have had a lot of "manure" dumped on me. I bet you have, too. We have had things happen to us that "smelled" horrible…things like failure, depression, broken dreams or relationships, and sin. Everyone's past is filled with awful, painful, and unpleasant experiences. We all wish we could go back and change areas where we messed up. We suffer from pain and shame. We fear our failures will lead us to destruction, and the more the manure piles up, the worse we feel about our ability to produce spiritual fruit.

No one wants to be permeated by the manure and rot of life; however, if we trust God, he can take all the pain and shame that plague our lives and turn it for good. God has a way of taking the muck and mire that life dishes out and using it to create something beautiful. Much like manure promotes plant growth, everything that we have been through has made us into the people that we are today. God can use all the pain and anger, the anguish and mistakes and failure to promote His kingdom.

Let us consider Saint Patrick, patron saint of Ireland. He is considered the greatest missionary to Ireland. As a young man he lived on the island of Ireland as a slave and knew its culture and way of life. After he escaped from slavery, he went into the ministry as a priest. He moved back into Ireland. Since he had grown up in the Irish culture, he was able to use what he had experienced to reach the lost people in Ireland. We, too, can use the things that have haunted us from the past to help us reach others.

For example, it is easier for an ex-drug addict to reach drug addicts than it is for those of us who have had no experience with drugs. Also, it is easier for a divorcee to minister to a group of divorced people than it is for someone who has been happily married for years. The things we have gone through qualify us to minister to others who have gone, or are going through, the same things we experienced. While some people say that God causes these problems as a way to promote growth, such problems and trials happen because of our mistakes and sins or the mistakes and sins of others. Nevertheless, God can take things that we go through, even the problems we had experienced before we were Christians and turn those negative experiences into a testimony of His glory.

In Revelation 12:10-11, John paints the picture of a courtroom. God stands as the judge in the court, and the devil is called the accuser of the believers. In verse ten the devil is described as making accusations to God against the believers both day and night. In the imagery here, as well as other places in the New Testament, Satan is represented as a prosecuting attorney, standing before the judge explaining why the defendant, or believer, is guilty.

John writes, "And they [believers] overcame him [Satan] by the blood of the lamb and by the word of their testimony." There are two things mentioned in this passage that aided the believers in overcoming the enemy's accusations. First, John says that they overcame the enemy by the blood of the Lamb, or the salvation work of Jesus Christ.

Next, they overcame the enemy by the word of their testimony. The enemy, as the accuser of the believers, attempts to show God that we should be convicted for our sins. In 1 Peter 5:8, the enemy is called the adversary, which is a term for a prosecuting attorney. No matter what accusations the accuser makes, we overcome those accusations by our testimony of God's redemptive power.

Several years ago, I was called upon to comfort a man who had lost a son in a tragic car accident. At first, I could not relate to his situation because I have never lost a child. However, in the middle of our conversation he mentioned that he no longer could trust a God who would allow this tragedy to happen. He was also angry at himself for not being able to be prevent the tragedy. This struck a chord in my heart, because I had been there before.

When we found out that my older son had a been through a very traumatic experience that had caused significant emotional damage to him, I found myself in the same place, asking God why He had allowed this to happen. I was a preacher, serving God daily, trusting Him to take care of us, yet He let my son experience something that no one should ever have to face. I also blamed myself, feeling like I should have known that something was happening and should have protected him better.

Renewing Nutrients

This commonality opened the opportunity for me to plant the seed of the Word in this man's heart. I believe that the Word of God does not return void, and so that seed was planted and will grow. My testimony was able to make a difference in his situation. What was "manure" in my life can be one of the greatest opportunities for growth in another person's spiritual life, if I allow God to use me by sharing that testimony with someone else.

What to do if manure is fresh?

As we mentioned a little bit ago, manure has a very strong smell and is very foul. Though manure can be one of the greatest organic fertilizers, it can be one of the greatest pollutants as well. Fresh cow manure is filled with bacteria that can contaminate the crop. It also is so strong that it can burn the plants and their roots.

Consequently, it is important for farmers to allow the manure to age. The length of composting can differ depending on the many different items being composted. By the time the compost product is ready, the odor has begun to fade, and the harmful contaminants have been replaced with vital nutrients for the soil.

Similarly, the pain that we live through can be harmful if it does not have time to cure. Before God can use our testimony to reach others, there must be a level of aging in us. The "manure" must age before it will increase our growth. Consider a minister stepping up to the pulpit on Sunday and saying, "While I was looking at internet porn last night, God told me that I was going to preach on pornography today." The minister would probably be reprimanded for his candidness and could even lose his job because the people might feel that he was unfit. On the other hand, if the minister had been free from pornography for a significant length of time, and he felt led to preach on the subject of pornography, the congregants would be more likely to listen intently because of the minister's experience.

Another common example is seen in twelve-step recovery organizations. People who have suffered with addictions such as alcoholism, drug abuse, etc. come together to help one another in the battle with addiction. When a person finds him or herself in a difficult situation, he or she can call the sponsor for help.

Nevertheless, a person who has only been sober a short period of time is not the best option to be a mentor for another addict. The person may not be strong enough to refrain from falling back into the same old habits. After he or she is in recovery and has developed techniques for continued growth, that person is more likely to be able to help someone else.

Likewise, before God can use us to minister to others, there must be a change. In the fifth chapter of Mark, the evangelist tells the story about Jesus entering an area where a demon-possessed man lived. He was so tormented that he did not know his family, no one could bind him, and he was naked and living in the tombs. Jesus spoke to the demons and cast them out. In Luke's account it says that when the people came out to see what had happened, they found the demoniac dressed and in his right mind sitting at Jesus' feet. There was a very definite change in his life. The people knew him as being crazy and destructive, but now they found him rational and cognizant. The formerly possessed man begged to go with Jesus.

Instead, Jesus instructed him to return to his home and his family. Though he would have had a great testimony, he was not spiritually ready.

Another very important change that we encounter in the Bible is found in the fourth chapter of John. Jesus and his disciples were passing through Samaria at noon, and as the disciples went in town to get food, Jesus found a woman who was coming to draw water from Jacob's Well. Normally, people would have drawn water in the cool of the day, but this woman was coming in the heat of the day to avoid being around the other women from town. Within just a few verses we find that she had a very shady past. Not only had she been married multiple times, the man she was now with was not her husband.

When she met Jesus, he showed her unconditional acceptance. Unlike the many other men who had used and abused her, Jesus showed her that she was valued. She discovered from this encounter that God loved her regardless of her past.

She ran back into town calling, "I've met a man." Everyone was probably thinking, "I bet you met a man; you meet a different one everyday…" But this time was different. Initially, the people in the community were skeptical of her testimony. The "manure" was not yet mature. Nevertheless, there was a change in this woman's behavior, so the crowds came out to meet Jesus.

In both Biblical examples we find that God can use our past to help others; however, we must first allow Him to make a difference in our lives. When we allow God to truly take all the areas of our lives and do a work in us, He can use our testimony to help us bear greater fruit in the future.

When He cleanses us, He can then use that pain or depression that we experienced as the fertilizer to stimulate spiritual growth in others.

Can we avoid nutrient theft?

After we have allowed God to begin the work of salvation in our lives, it is very important to continually avoid allowing the things of the world to pull us away. Many people do not realize that if a garden is planted too close to other vegetation such as bushes and trees, the bushes and trees steal the nutrients that were meant to be used for the garden. We must make sure that we are retaining the nutrients that we have worked so hard to build.

In the same way that there is nutrient theft in nature, there can also be spiritual nutrient theft. We must consider where we are planted right now. No one wants to admit that it is easy for friends and colleagues to be bad influences on us. Sadly, many Christians maintain the same friends that they had before they began building their relationship with Christ. Those same friends can have a very negative effect on us. When Jesus comes into our lives, we are no longer our own. We are bought with a price. In Matthew 5:14, Jesus said, "You are the salt of the earth…You are the light of the world." We provide the savor to spice up life, and we shine out his light in front of the world.

There are people who inadvertently pull us down spiritually. They may be negative and constantly ridiculing everything we do. Some people are like parasites that literally destroy the good things that God is doing in our lives. The enemy can use those people to get us involved in the ways of the world. However, there is the option to build new relationships with others. We can find people who are able to add to our spiritual growth.

Chapter 5 – Plant the Seed

A seed is an awesome part of a plant. It is usually incased in a fruit, and it can produce exponential growth by creating a plant that can bear fruit as well as other seeds. When the seed is put into good soil, it reacts to the water and the nutrients to produce roots and a stem. That stem will grow leaves and, ultimately, fruit. The fruit can then be used to produce more plants and then more fruit.

Why does a seed grow?

We mentioned earlier that we reap the fruit of the seeds we have sown. We will not get a banana from an apple tree or an onion from a tomato plant. Each seed has the DNA of the plant that it was taken from. In Mark 4:31-32, Jesus says, "[The Kingdom of God] is like a grain of mustard seed, which, when it is sown in the earth, is less than all of the seeds in the earth. But when it is sown, it groweth up, and becometh greater than all herbs, and shooteth out great branches, so that the fowls of the air may lodge under the shadow of it."

This example is given to demonstrate the power of faith, but it reminds us also that one of the smallest seeds in the world can grow a tree large enough that birds can rest in it. That little seed has the potential to become a mighty plant. Built deep inside a seed's DNA is everything that seed needs to bear fruit. It contains the potential to grow and increase its progeny by creating new seeds.

Correspondingly, each seed of the Word of God also has potential. Encased in every seed of the Word is the power to renew and develop us. Both the written and spoken Word of God have intrinsic energy. When God's Word goes forth, each Word is a seed that, if received and cultivated, will take root in our lives. That is why it is very important to respect the Word of God.

Proverbs 18:21 says that our words can contain the power of life or the power of death. As Christians we represent God, and so the things we say represent God to the world. Therefore, when words are spoken, they can be "fertilized" by faith and can bear fruit. If the words are positive and encouraging, their fruit will be positive and uplifting. If the words are negative and critical, their fruit will be destructive. It is all determined by us and how we use our words in our lives and the lives of others.

This can be clearly seen when we think about how words affect the development of children. Children who are ridiculed and abused, learn to believe the lies they are told and tend to suffer from a lower self-esteem. On the contrary, children who are encouraged and inspired tend to have a stronger self-esteem and personal confidence. Children live up to the standards they are given, and they believe what they are taught.

For this reason, we need to be more aware of the seeds that we are planting. When we speak the Word of God, or on behalf of God, we need to strive to help others. Furthermore, when we speak something out of anger or hurt someone with our words, it is important that we hold ourselves accountable and attempt to undo the damage we may have caused. In doing this, we choose to be representatives of Christ, working to build a world through love.

What are we planting?

I was told recently that I can improve the look of my yard by planting flowers that would grow throughout the year. Certain plants grow better in the spring, while others grow better in the fall. It was also advised that I can add evergreen plants to bring life even in the coldness of winter.

If we allow the Word of God to be a part of our lives, it becomes active in our times of need. No matter the season of life, or the problems we are going through, the Holy Spirit will always recall the right message at the right time. He can utilize the Word of God that has been planted inside our hearts.

Think about the seeds that we are planting. Every gardener must know what he or she is planting and what it will take to make the plants grow and thrive. We choose every day what we are going to plant that day. We plant into our lives with every word we say and everything we do. Encouraging words will bear happiness, while hateful and angry words bear depression. With faith we can build up ourselves and others, while fear and anguish can affectively destroy what we have worked so hard to maintain.

Since, our words do not only sow into our lives but into those around us, the more we speak into someone else's life, the greater effect those words can have on the other person. It is important to weigh our words before they leave our mouths. Even if a word was said in anger, all it takes is the empowerment of faith for that seed to take root and begin to grow in the lives of other people. Our words can be detrimental if we do not make sure we know what we are planting before we decide to sow.

In the book of Hosea, the people of God had moved far away from God. They chose to seek out foolishness, idolatry, and ultimately spiritual destruction through their rebellion and disobedience. In one passage, the Word gives the enigmatic statement, "For they that sow to the wind, reap a whirlwind."[12] The wind typically symbolizes something that is foolish and temporal. On the other hand, a whirlwind brings destruction and decimation. The people of Israel were foolishly sowing to their own destruction. In the same way, if we are unaware of the effects of our words and actions, we too, can sow destruction in our lives and the lives of others.

How are work and fruit related?

Looking back at the parable of the sower mentioned earlier, we recall that the sower planted the seeds in several different kinds of soil. As he scattered the seeds, some fell along the road, and the birds quickly swooped down and ate them up. Other seeds fell along the rocks where the soil was shallow. The plants sprang up quickly, but the sun quickly scorched them because they had no roots. Some fell among the thorns, and the thorns choked them out. Finally, the remaining seeds survived because they fell on good ground.

The disciples came to Jesus and asked the meaning of the parable. Jesus said to them that the soil along the roadway symbolized the people that who did not understand the Word of God, and the enemy swooped in

---

[12] Hosea 8:7

and snatched the seeds away. The soil along the stony ground represented those who received the Word quickly with enthusiasm, but because their faith was shallow, when they experienced life's difficulties, they lacked the spiritual depth to believe God's Word and support growth.

Furthermore, the soil filled with thorns signified sincere believers who readily accepted the Word of God, but the cares of life choked out their spiritual desire. Ultimately, the seed that fell upon the good ground represented those who allowed the seed not only to take root but grow into maturity. Jesus used these four different types of soil to describe everyone who has ever heard the Good News.

The Word of God is often used synonymously with God due to the verses in John 1 that refer to Christ as the Word. There is a much deeper theological truth here, but for the sake of this text we want to briefly state that the Word is the essence of God, just like a dandelion seed is the essence of a dandelion. When my daughter blows on a white dome-shaped dandelion, she watches with delight as all the small parachutes cascade across my yard. Since each of the little seeds contain what it was created to be, each seed has the potential to create a new plant. In the same way, as the essence of God is spoken forth, the Word can take root, grow, and develop in our lives. As we allow His Word to get inside of us through reading, studying, and hearing, the seeds will begin to create in us God's will.

Since the Word of God is vital to the Christian walk**,** one would assume God's Word would take a primary role in the life of Christians. Sadly, many Christians rarely open their Bibles. Many people who claim to follow God spend most of their lives ignoring the promises that God has made. For this reason, many people will never actually reach the potential that God has planned for them.

However, to truly bear spiritual fruit in our daily lives, we must do more than just hear or read God's Word. We must put it into practice. We remember Jesus' parable of the two builders; one of them built on rock and the other on the sand. Jesus compared their foundations to their willingness to put the Word into action. The man who founded his house upon the rock is like the person who actively incorporates the Word of God into life. The man who built his house on the sand was like a person who hears the Word but refuses to put it into practice.

The seed of the Word is not truly growing inside of us until we allow it to shine out in our lives. James 2:20 explains that an inactive faith is dead. He points out that many people say they have faith, but it is not evident in their lives. Consequently, if faith is not manifested in one's life, he or she effectively has no faith. If the Word is going to grow and produce fruit, there will be evidence in the person's life. If that evidence is not there, James says that the proposed faith does not exist.

How to ensure a future harvest?

A farmer does not eat all the fruit from the seed he plants. Instead, he or she sets aside some seed to plant the next year. If the farmer uses all the wheat that he grows, he will not have seed for the next planting season.

Recall the story in the first chapter about the water pump in the desert. The man had the option to drink the water for immediate satisfaction or use the water to produce more water for long-term abundance. If the farmer eats all the seed, he will have selfish immediate satisfaction. On the other hand, if he reserves some for planting, he will have food for the next year.

Most preachers describe "eating the seed" as not paying our offerings and tithes. Truthfully, if we do not give God his due, then we will have nothing to sow, "…give and it shall be given unto you." Nevertheless, anytime that we act out of selfishness, expending our resources and our energy on something for our own satisfaction we are eating the seed that could have been planted.

For instance, a talented singer that is singing for the world, chasing after the flesh, is eating his or her seed. A person seeking after the flesh instead of seeking after the Spirit eats the seed that he or she could be using for the kingdom of God. The difference is always the motive. Self-seeking is equal to the corruption of the flesh, while God-seeking is equal to the blessing of the Spirit.

PART 2
SPIRITUAL CULTIVATION

The stiff and wooden quality about our religious lives is a result of our lack of holy desire. Complacency is a deadly foe of all spiritual growth.[13]

--A.W. Tozer

---

[13] Tozer, A. W., *The Pursuit of God,* (Dallas, TX: Gideon House Books, 2017), p 4.

Chapter 6 – Maintain Growth

In the last chapter, we discussed the lack of spiritual evidence in the lives of many Christians. We looked at James' words relating to active faith and determined that inactive faith is really no faith at all.

In keeping with the idea of our plant metaphor, I am reminded about an old fichus tree that was found in a storage room a few years ago. It was covered in dust and debris and missing most of its leaves. At one time the tree was probably beautiful and stood erect in the corner of an office to bring a little appeal to a sterile environment. Sadly, when it was discovered with cobwebs blowing slightly in the breeze, it was worth nothing more than another piece of trash to be taken to the landfill.

Many Christians live their lives like that fichus, at one time vibrant and beautiful with its artificial leaves stretching out in all directions. However, it was packed away and forgotten, being left to rot in the back of a closet. In the same way, many people do not maintain their spiritual walk, leaving the stress and strain of the world to tarnish the luster that once existed in the their hearts. As it is with us all, if we do not maintain our relationship with Christ**,** we will not see spiritual growth. Even if the outside is polished and perfect, the inside may be rotted and diseased.

Maintain Growth

In the common drought-like conditions of West Texas, we have a problem that can exist with our outdoor plants. The plants may look healthy from the outside, but without proper maintenance they may not produce fruit. Sometimes even our native pecan trees will produce very small pecans due to the lack of nutrients throughout the year. Farmers must take this into account and work diligently to maintain growth or there will be no produce.

In the same way, to produce the fruit of the Spirit, we must maintain growth. We cannot sit around hoping that all is well, while slowly dying internally. Bearing fruit is more than just preparing the soil or planting the seed, we must take time to build a healthy relationship with God.

What necessities are needed for growth?

I am the king of killing plants. Unlike my children plants do not talk or run around. They sit in the same location all the time. I do not even notice that they are there. Soon the leaves begin to droop. Their tips begin to shrivel. Then the leaves begin to turn brown as the plant attempts to nourish its core. If I catch the plants at this phase, I might be able to save them. Typically, however, I miss the signs, and ultimately, the stems die, as do the roots. No amount of tender, loving, care will bring them back once the roots are dead.

One of the greatest signs of a fruit baring plant's health is the growth of fruit. When the plant is growing good fruit, it is healthy. On the contrary, if the fruit is bad or there is no fruit, the plant is not healthy and is lacking vital nutrients.

Our souls tend to experience this as well. At first, we may catch ourselves becoming less involved in the work of the church. Then we stop wanting to go to church. We find excuses and other things to do instead of being at church. Usually, if we catch it early, we can take care of our waning souls before we have wondered too far. Over time our hearts grow harder, and we no longer can feel the tug of God on our heart strings. Though, I do not believe in outright apostasy, or when a person moves too far away from God he or she cannot return, I do believe the farther we move away from Him, the harder it is for us to return.

King Saul was a mighty man of God. He loved God and righteously ruled the kingdom of Israel. For a while, He was the epitome of what a king should be. But, somewhere along the way Saul began to harden his heart toward God. He became disobedient. He did exactly what God told him not to. There came a point of no return in Saul's life. He no longer could make a connection with God. This led to his demise.

The spirit is just like the body; it needs nutrition. Some say, "I do not need to go to church, there are too many sinners and hypocrites." Do not worry; they have room for one more. We are all sinners, saved by grace. No one is perfect, and no one has the right to judge anyone else. If we do not want to be around sinners, we are saying we are better than the Lord Jesus Christ. Jesus spent all his time with sinners.

One important part of our spiritual walk is building relationships with other believers. By building spiritual relationships with others who believe like we believe, we will have people in our lives with whom we mutually rely for strength and encouragement. For this reason, it is important for us to find a church to become a part of.

If I visit a church, I typically know very quickly if it is a good fit for me and my family. Since there are many different churches, denominations, and affiliations, there is a church that can help fulfill anyone's needs. Also, when we are planted into a church, we can also provide for the needs of others.

Sadly, in our world of technology, television, and the internet, more and more people have "…forsaken the assembling of ourselves together".[14] They feel they can get everything they need from ministers online or over the airwaves. However, they miss out on the relationship-building that a fellowship of believers offers. We may not always agree with everyone in our spiritual circle. However, the opportunity to grow together and to work side-by-side helps to promote our spiritual welfare.

Another important aspect of church is the ministry of the Word. God gives the inspiration to the ministers. It is the Word that we need to hear. Feed upon the Word. In John 6:48, Jesus said, "I am the bread of life." Our spirits are nourished by Him.

We also feed upon the Word of God, found in the Bible. Psalms 119:105 says that God's Word is the lamp unto our feet and the light unto our paths. In Psalms 1, it says that the righteous always meditate upon the commandments of the Lord. This verse simply means to continually bring the God's Word to mind. We should never just read the Bible for the sake of reading it; instead, we need to learn and study the Word. The more we put the Word into our hearts, the more it affects us, allowing us to apply it to our daily lives.

Romans 12:2 says, "Being not conformed to the mindset of this age but being transformed with a renewed mind." Paul begs us to abandon the mindset of the world and allow our minds to be renewed. This is difficult.

---

[14] Hebrews 10:25

We are used to thinking like the world. We grew up around people who had the same mindset. Nevertheless, it is important to allow God to free us from that way of thinking and to transform us through renewing our minds by the power of the Word of God.

What if I am not in an optimal place for growth?

While driving here in Texas, we pass many farms with large irrigation systems used to carry water over great distances. Methods of irrigation have been passed down since ancient times. In Ecclesiastes 2:6, the wise man speaks of digging ponds to help provide water for the crops. In Deuteronomy 11:10, the writer compares the land of Promise to the land of Egypt, by saying that the Promised Land has abundance and is not like Egypt where they had to irrigate the crops. Any time the crops are not able to get the needed water from nature, the caretakers must obtain water artificially.

Maybe we live or work in an environment where we are not fed spiritually on a regular basis. Maybe we work around people who are constantly angry and hateful, possibly even derogatory toward our Christian beliefs. It is important to irrigate our spirits. We need to find ways to feed our spirits even when our environment is working to tear them down. The only way that we can maintain healthy spiritual growth is through finding a way of feeding our souls in a world of spiritual famine.

How do I avoid things that prevent growth?

Over the past several years, I have helped pull the weeds in our church flower beds. I learned after the first time that I need to wear proper protection, and I need the proper tools to remove the weeds. Weeds are tough. Many have thorns and burrs. They want to stay in the ground. Weeds are some of the fastest growing plants. One plant grows, and within a few days it can overrun the yard. We always must watch for weeds.

Look back at the parable of the sower. When the seeds fell among the thorns, the thorns quickly grew up and choked them out. They stole the water and nutrients from the seedlings and strangled them. The thorns represent the problems that destroy a person's hope. If we allow other things to choke out the Word of God in us, the seed will not grow.

Sin spreads weeds among the seed implanted inside of us. It can quickly spread, causing damage everywhere it grows. Much like we think of a rumor spreading like wildfire when it gets started, any sin can spread and leave destruction in its wake. When we allow weeds to spread throughout our hearts, even our good intentions can be choked out. If sin can take hold of us, it takes the place of the Word of God and crowds out the hope that we find in Him.

When we are pulling weeds, it is always important to pull up the roots with the weeds. If we don't, the roots can begin to grow and spread even when there is no visible plant. If we use soil that contains weed roots, they can continue to grow. The weed starts below the surface and cannot be seen without digging deeper. Sin does not begin with noticeable signs and temptation begins with small roots that grow beneath the surface of our hearts.

Several years ago, there was a Christian movie produced call *Fireproof*. In the movie the main actor had a problem with pornography. The movie demonstrated how that sin caused the relationship with his wife to deteriorate. Throughout the story he learned how to overcome the secret hidden aspects of sin and began building a deep and loving relationship with his wife.

In the same way, sin does not start in an obvious manner; it is a slow process that starts with small steps that can be easily hidden from view. Over time, if it is not dealt with, sin can easily take hold and grow into a lifestyle. Nevertheless, if we choose to deal with the roots before they can grow, we can remove the problem before it has a chance to take control.

We must be aware of the enemy and his work, so that we can catch the weeds as soon as they sprout. In the same way, we need to immediately stamp out the enemy's foothold in our lives. When temptation comes, we learn to refuse it. When the chance and desire to sin present themselves to us, we should choose to go the other direction. Escaping temptation is not a cowardly move because it takes more boldness and self-control to run from sin than it takes to follow the crowd and embrace it.

Joseph, in the book of Genesis, had the chance to have an affair with his owner's wife. If he had done it, she would have taken care of him, provided for him, and been his "sugar mama". He would have been rich and prosperous. But he ran away so fast that he left his cloak behind.

The woman lied about him and he was punished even though he did not sin. But by the end of his life he was much better off than he would have been had he given in to temptation. He was even able to save the lives of his family members in the midst of a famine.

There is nothing wrong with running from sin. God honors those that refuse to disobey Him. He glorifies those who humble themselves and rely on Him. When the weeds of sin begin to break through the ground of our minds, we need to destroy them before they have a chance to grow.

What if I do not see an immediate change?

Many times, when people do not see an immediate difference, they "dig up their seed." Many people have the mindset that when they ask God for something, He will move immediately, and when it takes longer, they feel that God has refused to answer the prayer.

A farmer does not plant a seed in the ground and the next day run out and dig up the seed and throw it away because it is not growing. Nevertheless, many Christians receive prayer on their behalf on a Sunday morning and the next morning get up and say, "I am still so sick; the prayer did not work." Instead of trusting God and waiting on Him, we throw out every seed that we plant when we let our faith waver.

I once heard a person come for prayer one week, and then the next Sunday she came back for prayer for the same thing. I was amazed by what she said. Most people would blame God for not receiving an answer, but she said, "I wavered. The next morning when the symptoms were still there, I allowed my faith to falter instead of trusting that God was doing His work." Amazingly, she recognized that she had faltered in her faith instead of blaming God. Instead of holding fast to the Lord and the seed that she planted by faith, she allowed herself to struggle, and she knew it. It demonstrates our spiritual maturity when we can recognize our mistakes.

Correspondingly, one of the things that the Lord taught me very early in my ministry was to be careful what I said after I prayed for people. I caught myself praying for someone and believed with faith that God was working on his or her behalf. Then when someone asked how the person was doing, I would practically destroy everything that I had just prayed for. I would pray for a person in the hospital, then when someone would ask, I would say, "He's not doing very well." I believe we must be realistic and honest, but what a kick in the faith!

When we speak the Word in faith, we cannot immediately go dig it back up, just because we do not see an instantaneous difference. Instead, while speaking the Word of faith, we should nurture it and let it take root deep inside. For instance, even when we do not immediately see the miracle, we must know that God is still working behind the scenes.

On the contrary, I am not telling someone to lie to him or herself and live in denial. I know a person that truly believed that all illness was in the head and that by speaking of the illness, he was acknowledging its existence. Part of trusting in God begins by accepting that there is a problem and believing that God is more than capable of taking care of it.

As we continue in our spiritual growth, it is important for us to avoid things that we know pull us away from God. Whether it be people, situations, or our own lack of trust that causes our faith to waver, we must learn ways to promote spiritual growth. For growth in our relationship with Christ, we must be willing to wait patiently on God. No matter how hard we try in our own abilities, we cannot overcome sin. When we allow God to take control, we will see change.

Chapter 7 – Pruning Away Decay

In the last chapter we ended by discussing the need for the consistent caretaking of our spiritual lives. Another area that requires maintenance that we have not discussed yet is the act of pruning. There are times in the life of a tree when branches must be removed to help the tree grow, but if done improperly, pruning can destroy the health that we are attempting to improve. In this section we will be looking at the importance of allowing God to remove certain things from our lives to bring increase. Although, this is one of the most difficult parts of the growth process, it is necessary for our continued spiritual health.

Why do we have to prune?

In John 15:1, Jesus sat at the last supper talking with his disciples. He begins the discourse by saying, "I am the true vine, and my father is the husbandman." Over the next several verses, He goes on to explain the relationship between the vine and the branches. In verse 2, He explains that the husbandman, or vinedresser, removes the branches that do not bear fruit, but He prunes the branches that bear fruit, so they can increase their production.

For the health of trees, it is important to remove branches that are dead or diseased. When a tree has insect-infested limbs, it is important to cut away those limbs before the infestation extends to the rest of the tree. If the limbs are not receiving the much-needed nutrients, the limbs will die and will ultimately break loose. This can cause injury to the tree and damage to the items around the tree. However, removing dead and diseased limbs before they break loose from a tree will help protect the integrity of the tree.

Additionally, pruning promotes growth and fruit production. We have discussed in depth that a tree first supports its trunk and branches before it can support fruit. The more branches a plant must support, the more the nutrients will be expended. Cutting back unneeded branches frees up extra nutrients for the tree to increase fruit productivity. For this reason, tree farmers will annually cut back the lower branches on their trees.

Much in the same way, there are things in our lives that need to be removed for us to be able to grow and produce the fruit that we were created to produce. Pruning can be a very painful process. It forces us to leave our comfort zone by eliminating areas that we may not have previously been willing to deal with. Nevertheless, once we are willing to let those things be removed, fruit will begin to grow, replacing the disease and decay that were cut out.

What is being pruned?

There are many things in our lives that can lead us to temptation. I recently was talking to a parishioner who had been in a sexual relationship with her boyfriend. She said that she wanted to straighten out her life but did not know how. I told her that one of the first steps she needed to take was to do something about the improper relationship that she had with her boyfriend. Since sin separates us from God, the nature of her relationship was effectively creating a chasm between her and God.

Another temptation that many deal with is pornography. Pruning that limb can be especially difficult. I have worked with people who had to make a commitment to stay away from the internet forever because of the temptation to view pornographic material. I also have friends and family who are unwilling to watch television and movies that have certain ratings because the situations they find there are very familiar and can easily entice them to return to a life of sin.

If a person is controlled by a certain vice, it is important to avoid that sin at all cost. A recovering alcoholic learns during treatment that all it takes is one drink for the cycle of alcoholism to begin again. A person who struggles with excessive spending and increased debt knows that it only takes a credit card offer in the mail to lead to the temptation to spend more. For many people, one small, seemingly innocent, action can lead to a destructive relapse.

I tell the youth at the church, "If your friends cause you sin, then find new friends." At one time we had several couples in the youth group. It seemed like optimal situation because they were only together at chaperoned church functions. Within a short period of time we noticed their relationships were strained, and several of the individuals appeared to be suffering. After talking with the youth involved, we discovered that they were struggling with the commitments they had made to remain sexually pure. Before it was too late, they realized that the only way to maintain that commitment was to separate. We hate to admit it, but there are times that we need to change our friendships or break up relationships to help us avoid the temptations the relationships are leading us into.

Second Timothy 2:22 says, "Flee also youthful lusts." The Greek word for "flee" means to "run away from" or "retreat". As we discussed with the example of Joseph in chapter 6, there is nothing wrong with running away from an evil situation. We should not knowingly put ourselves into settings that will lead to temptation. For instance, a couple cannot have sex if they are never left alone together. A person cannot get drunk if he or she chooses to avoid alcohol. If we are not strong enough to abstain, we should choose to be wise enough to run the other direction.

How is pruning accomplished?

Self-pruning is the least-painful pruning there is. If we are willing to make a difference in our own lives and willingly remove things that we know are causing us to fall into temptation, we will not have to go through the harsher pain of being pruned by God. It may hurt, but with God's help we can overcome the pain. In Mark 9:43, Jesus says, "If your hand offendeth thee cut it off." Likewise, the scripture goes on to talk about the foot and the eye in the same manner. It is better to enter the Kingdom of God without something that we consider vital, such as a hand, foot, eye, or even a relationship, than to hold onto the item and end up in Hell because of it.

We need to make a differentiation between self-pruning and legalism. Becoming self-disciplined in an area is very different than believing that one's actions can constitute, or add to, the work of grace on the cross. I was taken aback by a discussion I heard some time ago.

Someone argued that self-pruning was a form of attempting to earn salvation instead of relying fully upon the cross for redemption.

If we believe that salvation is based on what we can accomplish on our own, we render the cross of Christ unnecessary. Such people feel that their works are required to add to the sacrifice of Christ, which basically means that what Jesus did on the cross was insufficient to bring salvation. Furthermore, if people begin restricting their actions as an attempt to be closer to God, those people can easily believe themselves to be more deserving of God's grace than others. We call this act of self-righteousness, legalism.

Acts of legalism have created divisions in churches and formed denominations among groups of people. Paul spoke extensively about legalism in the book of Galatians and mentioned it many times in his other writings. While restricting one's actions may cause the person to feel more spiritual or make him or her seem more spiritual to others, it is actually a sign of spiritual immaturity. In other words, if we cannot trust God to truly save us through His act of grace on the cross, we lack faith.

On the other hand, if a person chooses to regulate different parts of his or her life because the person knows that it may lead to sin, that is his or her own discipline. God may put on someone's heart that he or she should break off a close relationship because that relationship is leading in the wrong direction. Others may feel that God is telling them to avoid alcohol as a technique to avoid temptation. Such decisions are on a personal level, and God can use them to build faith and self-control.

I believe there are basically two ways that self-pruning crosses over into legalism. First, when a person believes that his or her acts directly supplement the work of Christ in salvation, it becomes legalism. When someone chooses to live a certain way because it makes him or her to feel holier, it is no longer simply a self-discipline. In addition, if a person, or group believes that everyone should partake in a specific discipline or risk losing salvation, that attitude is legalistic.

Learning self-control and self-discipline is part of the Christian life. It is made possible to us through the act of the cross. We are not able to do it alone, but through the power of the Spirit of God. No matter how hard we try, we cannot truly discipline ourselves without the help of God. However, we can choose to be willing to let God work in us.

How does God Prune?

There are several ways that God prunes our spiritual lives. Revelation 3:19 says, "As many as I love, I rebuke and chasten." He prunes because He loves us and wants the best for us. I discipline my children not because I want to hurt and abuse them, but because I would rather address my children's actions while they are young instead of letting them end up in trouble because I chose not to be a parent. Discipline is an act of love. I do not like to discipline my children. There are times that I must make decisions that hurt me as much as it hurts them, but for their own good, I choose to discipline them. Similarly, God chooses to prune us because He loves us.

The most common method of pruning is through reading God's Word. The more we read and know the Word, the more we can exemplify that word in our lives. If we allow His Word to make a difference in us, then we allow ourselves to be changed. Moreover, He also uses the Word through preaching and counseling to help prune away the areas of decay from our lives.

When the Word is coming forth, we need to allow God to make a difference inside. He helps us to develop the nature of Christ and overcome sin. His Spirit works in us to prune away things that are not of God. This pruning helps us develop a deeper relationship with God and promotes spiritual growth.

Another type of natural pruning also occurs as the power of God changes our lives. Many new Christians have friendships and relationships that naturally dissolve as the new believer gets closer to God. The changes in a person's life dissuade the negative friendships, and unhealthy relationships may disappear without much effort. People who are unwilling to accept Christ are often uncomfortable when a friend no longer seeks things of the flesh. God is then able to provide new friends and relationships that complement the new believer's spiritual journey.

The more painful pruning comes when we are not willing to allow God to prune us. We all have areas in our lives that we do not want God to touch, so we fight against Him. Nevertheless, God loves us enough to remove areas even though He knows the pain that pruning will cause.

For instance, I met a gentleman who went through a bitter divorce due to his continual infidelity. God worked with him for years to end the affair, but he felt he could not walk away. The day came that his wife found out about his adulterous acts; it cost him his family and his relationship with most of his friends. He not only no longer had a wife, but he also no longer had the girlfriend. After all was said and done, he was able to admit that it took an act of God to end his life of promiscuity. Sadly, it also cost him dearly.

This scenario leaves a big question, was it God's will to ruin his marriage? The man did not believe so. He knew that his actions had consequences. Every time he chose to participate in an action that broke his marriage vows, he knew what he was risking. If he had denied the illicit relationship in the beginning, his life would have been completely different; instead, he continued to sow to the flesh until it was too late.

God works out His will in us because we are willing to follow Him. He works within us, altering our paths and helping us to grow. But when He sees something that is hindering growth, He first tries to work through His Word, allowing the Spirit to make the changes. The Word comes to us from preachers and counselors, as well as, directly from the Bible, but change can only occur by the help of the Spirit. As a last resort God reaches down and changes the situation. He does this only because He loves us so much that He wants to spend eternity with us. That is why He died for us.

Can pruning cause damage?

A few years ago, we lived in a house with a very large oak tree in the front yard. It was full of low-hanging branches, and we discovered that we could be fined if it began impeding traffic. I contacted a tree trimmer who had spent many years learning about the proper technique for maintaining and protecting trees. I wanted to ensure that we did not damage the tree in any way by cutting off some of the limbs.

This arborist told me that the best time to cut back the tree was in the winter when the tree has the most resources in reserve. He also recommended trimming small branches and avoid cutting the larger primary branches. If we attempted to remove the large heavy branches or to trim the branches during seasons of growth, it could send the tree into shock. If the tree went into shock, it could die.

When God is pruning back the needed areas of our lives, He is very willing to work with us. He could immediately remove all problem areas at once, but the damage that it could cause might outweigh the benefits. Instead, God is patient; He is slow to anger and rich in love.[15] His goal is to take care of us and help us, not cause us emotional shock.

Furthermore, we should also understand that other Christians are not going to change overnight. It is easy for seasoned Christians to feel superior to other Christians whom they feel are not maturing fast enough. Some people feel it is their duty to prune other Christians. They find something wrong in a person's life and then make it their life's mission to prune it out.

As a pastor I am called to present the Word of God, and if there is a persistent problem, I can confront that problem in a counseling setting and offer help. Even with presenting the Word of God and counseling, it is the Spirit's position and responsibility to work in people's lives. Pruning is a personal work that can only be accomplished with the help of the Spirit.

In Matthew 7:3, Jesus speaks to those who try to remove problems in other people's lives. He says, "Why beholdest thou the mote that is in thy brother's eye, but considerest not the beam that is in thine own eye?" In other words, Jesus asks, "Why do you notice the splinter that is in your brother's eye but pay no attention to the log that is in your own eye." We all have things that are in our lives that we need to remove. What then, gives us the right to try to remove the problems that other people have? Jesus

---

[15] Psalms 145:8

goes on to tell us that we need to remove the beam from our own eye so that we can help our brother with his.

The difference is our frame of mind. If we think it is our place to prune others, our vision is hindered by our pride and judgmental nature, which is of the flesh. Any time we look at someone in disdain, it is from the flesh not from the Spirit.

We must first remove our log of pride and judgment, and then we can see clearly how to help a fellow Christian to remove the splinter that's causing him or her problems. When we see clearly, we can offer prayer and support, but know that it is the work of the Holy Spirit to bring about change.

Chapter 8 – Purging the Chaff

In the last chapter, we used John 15:2 to introduce the idea of pruning or removing the things in our lives that cause us not to reach our potential ability to bear fruit. We discussed ways that we can willingly allow things to be removed from our lives. We also examined times when we do not willingly allow God to remove certain beliefs or activities or habits, and so He must step in more aggressively, which can be more painful for us.

In this chapter we are going to look at the Biblical idea of purging. While purging is often used synonymously with pruning, purging takes on a nature of judgment. In John 15:6, Jesus said, "If a man abides not in me, he is cast forth as a branch and is withered, and men gather them and cast them into the fire and they are burned."

Here, Jesus is still using the allegory of branches from a vine. If the branch is not abiding on the vine because it has been removed from the vine, there is nothing left but for it to be cast into the fire. Near my wife's work there was large tree with many low-hanging branches and dead limbs lying on the ground. It seemed that someone had pulled down the branches but never picked them up. Month after month she watched as the branches lay in the grass. Shortly before Christmas, we took the pickup truck and loaded up the branches. Time had cured them, and they were perfect for burning in our fireplace. In the same way, if we are not willing to allow God to prune away the old, dying parts of our lives, God is left with no other option but to remove the branches, Himself, and cast them into the fire.

In Matthew 3:7-9, John the Baptist was talking to a group of religious people. He was standing on the shore of the Jordan, baptizing, when he noticed some of the religious leaders coming to be baptized. He asked them, "O generation of vipers, who hath warned you to flee from the wrath to come? Bring forth therefore fruits meet for repentance: and think not to say within yourselves, we have Abraham as *our* father: for I say unto you, that God is able of these stones to raise up children unto Abraham." These individuals were seemingly some of the most religious people in Israel. They knew the Law and everything that it required of them, and as children of Abraham, they believed that they were saved simply because of their inheritance as Jews.

Between Malachi in the Old Testament and Matthew in the New Testament, many very important traditions emerged in the Jewish faith. First, they developed a smaller assembly called the synagogue that was much like the churches that we attend. In the synagogues, Jewish believers would meet and be taught by a religious leader such as a Rabbi. They would also spend time reading the Hebrew version of the Bible called the Tanak, which included the books of the Old Testament.

Secondly, there was also a growing rift among the Jews which prompted the creation of many different sects in Judaism. Of these, the most common sects that are mentioned in the New Testament were in opposition to one another in belief and practice: the Pharisees and the Sadducees. For instance, The Pharisees believed in an afterlife, especially a physical resurrection, while the Sadducees did not believe in privilege and punishment in the afterlife. Moreover, while both groups believed in the Law, or Torah, the Pharisees also believed in the oral traditions, while the Sadducees refuted them as non-authoritative. Such opposing views led to chaos within New Testament Judaism.

The religious people of the New Testament abandoned the true statutes of the Word of God. They interpreted the Law to meet their own desires and ignored the parts that convicted them of their sins. They missed the truth that God intended when the Law was instituted. It was never about a person's ability to serve God and earn righteousness; rather, it dealt with the change that God makes inside a person's heart.

Going back to the text in Matthew 3:10-12, John the baptizer goes on to say, "And now also the axe is laid unto the root of the trees: therefore, every tree which bringeth not forth good fruit is hewn down and cast into the fire. I indeed baptize you with water unto repentance: but he that cometh after me is mightier than I, whose shoes I am not worthy to bear: he shall baptize you with the Holy Ghost, and *with* fire: Whose fan *is* in his hand, and he will thoroughly purge his floor, and gather his wheat into the garner; but he will burn up the chaff with unquenchable fire."

When God instituted His commands in the Old Testament, he did so to teach the Jewish nation how to live. When building a relationship with God, we bear fruit. In the same way, the Old Testament believers also bore fruit. People like Abraham, Isaac, and Jacob had built relationships with God, and it was evident in their lives even before the Law was put in place.

By the New Testament time, in interpreting the Torah, or Law, the religious leaders amended and added to many of the commandments. The Pharisees, specifically, expanded many laws by adding multiple categories and subcategories to different parts of the Torah, for the primary goal of earning God's approval and controlling the populace.

Even with these expanded regulations, the hearts of the religious leaders drew farther and farther away from God. For this reason, John said, "…every tree which bringeth not forth good fruit is hewn down and cast into the fire." The religious individuals were not bringing forth good fruit, so John wanted to warn them of the coming judgment.

What does the Word mean by fire?

In Matthew 3:10-12, John the Baptist uses the Greek word *"pur"* three times meaning fire. Here John the Baptist uses two different images. First, he uses the idea of a tree that is not bearing good fruit being cut down and burned. Then he uses the image of Jesus as a thresher, "whose fan is in his hand" purging the floor, gathering the wheat, and preparing to burn up the chaff. In both of these allusions the Baptizer is relating fire to judgment and purging. The word *"pur"* literally means fire, and it is used other places as a means of judgment and a destructive purifying force.[16] While in the Greek language *"pur"* is used for fire, similarly in Latin the word *"pur"* means pure. These roots have been transformed in other languages like English to describe the act of purification.

In this case, John is using the term "fire" as a purifying judgment. In the first image God is judging the trees that bear bad fruit, and in the second image the thresher is purifying the wheat by separating and burning up the chaff. What John is trying to tell them is that Jesus Christ would

---

[16] Friberg, Timothy, Barbara Friberg, and Neva F. Miller. *Analytical Lexicon of the Greek New Testament*. Vol. 4 of Baker's Greek New Testament library, (Grand Rapids: Baker Books, 2000), p 339.

bring the baptism of the Holy Spirit and purifying fire. We can render this as a final judgment (the axe is at the root of the tree) or judgment through purification (thoroughly purging his floor).

In Isaiah 4:2-4, the writer speaks of the glorious day of the Lord. He says, "…the Lord shall have washed away the filth of the daughters of Zion and shall have purged the blood of Jerusalem from the midst thereof by the spirit of judgment, and by the spirit of burning." Purging is a form of judgment. It is judging and removing a small part to protect the whole. As mentioned in the last chapter, pruning a tree is a way of removing diseased and dead branches for the sake of the whole tree. Likewise, purging is the Holy Spirit's way of removing things from our lives that we need not have. And that purging can be accomplished only by the Spirit.

While there are areas of weakness that we can prune through the strength of God such as breaking habits or avoid negative relationship, there are some areas that only the Holy Spirit can purge. True deliverance and healing can only be achieved through the power of the Spirit of God. The Holy Spirit is the sustainer of God's providence in our lives and empowers us by helping us to live daily.

As the Holy Spirit does a work in our lives, we begin to develop better actions. These actions are the manifest work that God created us to achieve. In Ephesians 2:8-10, Paul says, "For by grace are ye saved through faith; and that not of yourselves: *it is* the gift of God: Not of works, lest any man should boast." But not ending there, he continues to say, "For we are his workmanship, created in Christ Jesus unto good works, which God hath before ordained that we should walk in them." Even though we are not saved by our good works; good works are a byproduct of being saved.

Without the work of the Spirit in our lives we would not be able to live the Christian life.

What does the fire accomplish?

The flesh is the carnal nature which seeks after things of the flesh. The Holy Spirit brings the spiritual nature which seeks after the things of the Spirit. For millennia fire has been used for purification. During plagues homes were burned to end the spread of the disease. Early medics used fire to cleanse and cauterize wounds. It burned away the flesh of the sacrifice in the Old Testament. The Holy Spirit burns in us to remove everything that is not of God.

We find another example in the refinement of precious metals. Gold by itself is a very pliable material which can be easily molded. When gold is mined, it is filled with impurities that must be removed before the gold can be used in manufacturing. When gold is melted, the impurities, or dross, rise to the top and can then be easily skimmed off. Gold cannot be purified without being tried in the fire.

Similarly, there are areas of our lives that need to be removed in order for us to truly live a Christian life. We carry around garbage, and it affects how we live. Since human nature is at enmity with God, it wars against God. But the Spirit sets us at peace with God. It burns away all of the things of the flesh, destroying the yoke of the enemy.

Who is judging me?

Judgment will come to everyone's door, but we are the one who decides who does the judging. Either we judge ourselves now and deal with our sins, or God will judge us later. On the Day of Judgment, it is too late for us to judge ourselves. We have to allow the Spirit to help us become aware of our imperfections. There are things that we cannot change in ourselves, but the Spirit gives us strength. Philippians 4:13 does not say, "I can do all things because I am strong on my own." It says, "I can do all things through Christ who strengtheneth me."

There is a difference between living a perfect life and being a Christian. A perfect life is determined by statutes, while a Christian life is forged by forgiveness. Jesus was talking to the scribes and Pharisees in Matthew 23:25-28. The teachers of the Torah lived a perfect life according to the Law, but hidden deep inside were filled with corruptible sins. He said that they cleaned the outside of the cup and saucer but left the inside dirty. Metaphorically, He also said that they were like beautiful tombs painted white but filled with death inside.

As followers of Christ, our goal should never be to act perfectly. Rather, we need to live our lives like the forgiven sinners that we are. We cannot allow ourselves to take on a self-righteous outward appearance and resemble something that we are not. Instead, what the world sees of us must reflect what we are in Christ. Similarly, that should also be whom we see when we look in the mirror.

Moreover, we cannot wear a different mask depending on where we are. We cannot wear one face when we are with our secular friends and another when we are with our Christian friends. The world must see the same person that God sees. All masks and false personas must be burned away.

In other words, the refining power of God burns away the chaff that remains inside all of us. As the fleshly nature that we hold on to is surrendered to God, it is overcome by the purifying power of His spirit. It is only through His power that our lives are refined, taking the pieces that are broken and making them new. God's Spirit shows us the areas of our life that are filled with decay and brings to light any darkness inside our hearts so that we can clearly see.

Chapter 9 – Harvest Time

Finally, at the end of the growing season, comes the time for harvest. Galatians 6:9-10, "And let us not be weary in well doing: for in due season we shall reap, if we faint not. As we have therefore opportunity, let us do good unto all men, especially unto them who are of the household of faith." It is so easy to lose faith when we do not see immediate results. We do not see everything that God sees.

How do I keep going if I am not seeing expected results?

At the beginning of my pastoral ministry I had the opportunity to work in the youth department. I have to say, there were times that I truly felt it was pointless. I taught them the Word and ministered the best way that I knew how, but there was no sign of growth. Then, when I finally decided, "That is it, I have had enough", one of the young men told me that he felt he was called to the ministry. I had felt everything I said was going in one ear and out the other, but God's Word was not going to return void. It was making a difference.

Through the tough times it is very hard. A farmer does not go out the day after he plants his seeds looking to see if the seeds are growing. He does not return a week later to see if the plant has produced fruit. Every farmer knows that it takes time. There is a time of growth, a time of maturation, and a time of harvest.

During the growing season we must not lose heart. We must make it through that period of time before we can see the fruit mature. The fruit needs to mature before we can harvest it. The word says in Ecclesiastes 3:11, "He hath made everything beautiful in its time." We typically take that to mean in God's time, but truly it means in the proper time that is most appropriate for growth. God is not growing us in His time, but in the proper time for our sake. He will not attempt a harvest before we are ready.

For instance, when I was fresh out of high school, my pastor told me that he felt it was time for me to begin my preaching ministry. I was very excited, but I waited, and nothing became of it. I went to my first two years in college and, like many young students, hit some rough patches. I bounced around from school to school, trying to find my niche. I also was in a relationship that I was sure would last forever but ended with me nursing a broken heart.

Several years later, after I was married, and our first child had been born, the day came when I was finally asked to preach. Later, when I spoke with my pastor about his earlier statement regarding my readiness to begin my preaching ministry, he replied, "When you first graduated and went off to college, several things happened-that made me realize that you needed more growth before you entered the pulpit. Looking back now, I can fully agree with him.

How do I know what I am reaping?

In my Grandmother's family were many migrant workers. They made a living by travelling around to different places working on farms. They would reap the bountiful harvest that others had grown. Many migrant families travel around throughout the year knowing which fruits would be ready for harvesting at the different times of the year.

A farmer is not surprised at the crop that he is growing. He plants with purpose, choosing seeds for the plants that he intends to grow. Sadly, many times as Christians, we sow at random and then are surprised by what we reap. For instance, a person may speak out in judgment against a fellow Christian and then be surprised when the person being judged leaves the church, hurt and alone. Other times, an individual strikes out in anger frequently, and then wonders why people decline an invitation to attend church. Our words and our actions affect the lives of others, and we are responsible for the consequences of those actions.

On the other hand, we sometimes sow positively into a person's life and are then surprised when God uses that act of kindness to bring a much-needed change. Furthermore, some Christians give to a ministry and are surprised when God brings the increase. As followers of Christ we should not be surprised when we reap what we sow. Whether we sow good or bad, we will reap the consequence of our actions. Therefore, we should be careful to sow the kind of seed that will produce the harvest we are wanting.

God's Word does not return to Him void, and we will reap what we have sown. When you sow to the flesh, you harvest things that are corruptible. The flesh only reaps that which is perishable. Sex before marriage may provide a temporary satisfaction, but it will reap pain and heartache. By the same token, allowing one's job to dominate his or her life may provide an envious way of life, but it can reap emptiness, loneliness, and frustration. Everything the world has to offer may seem to satisfy the "here and now," but it will ultimately yield destruction.

If you sow righteousness, then you will reap eternity. We sow righteousness by allowing the Lord to work in our lives, because through the sacrifice of Jesus Christ at Calvary, we have become the righteousness of God. Our personal righteousness is nothing but filthy rags in God's sight, but Jesus cleansed us so that when we stand before the Father, we will appear spotless.

What is it like when the harvest comes?

Amos spoke to the Northern Kingdom of Israel sometime around 765-750 BC. He was not a prophet, nor was he the son of a prophet. He was a shepherd and tender of the sycamore trees. Amos did not live his entire life wanting to minister for God. He did not desire to be a prophet, but he was the called by God. For this reason, he proclaimed the Word of the Lord.

God gave him a very strong proclamation for the northern ten tribes of Israel. By the time that Amos was called to minister, the people of the Northern Tribes had become greedy, heaping the blessings of God upon themselves to fulfill their own lusts. In the book of Amos, he makes several startling accusations. For instance, Amos chapter eight speaks of the wealthy people lending money to the poor people so they could buy sandals. When the poor could not repay, the rich members of society would take the debtors captive and sell them as slaves. Amos chapter 6 speaks of the gluttons who would recline on their expensive couches and have lambs and calves butchered as a delicacy instead of letting the animals mature so they could provide meat for several families. Little did the people know, they were about to be taken into captivity by the Assyrians because of the atrocities they had committed due to their selfish pride.

In the very last chapter of the book of Amos, God makes a very strong promise to his people. It says in Amos 9:13, "Behold, the days come, saith the Lord, that the plowman shall overtake the reaper, and the treader of grapes him that soweth seed." In the restoration of the people of God they will lack nothing because the harvest will be so great that the reapers will still be harvesting when it is again time to plow. Also, the treaders of the grapes will still be trying to tread the grapes when the sowers are planting new seeds. It will be a time of plenty.

Since they were being taken into captivity, the people of God had every reason to believe they would never see their homes again. After the Northern tribes were taken by the Assyrians and the Southern tribes by the Babylonians, they were without hope. There was nothing left for them. Their cities were destroyed; other people were brought in to replace them in the land as a symbol of their captivity, and it all happened as a result of their own sins. In Psalms 137:2, we read that they hung up their harps on the willow trees and would no longer sing the worship songs of their home because of the despair people felt. Nevertheless, the day of God's restoration would come.

What if I mess up?

The Jews reaped the judgment of the Lord because they forsook his statutes. For them it was a repeated problem. The Jews would commit to following God wholly, and God would bless them. They would then become self-serving and turn away from God, which would lead to destruction. The people would then realize what they had done and would return to God, beginning the cycle all over again.

Following Amos' predictions, the people were in despair in exile and captivity. However, the day came when God's people could return to the city of Zion. They rebuilt the temple, and they rebuilt the walls. They began living a normal Jewish life again. At first, they remained in the control of their pagan captors, but after a revolution, they enjoyed around a hundred years of independence before the Roman Empire moved into the Holy Land.

After the Romans conquered the Middle East, another divine promise was fulfilled. Around 6 B.C., a baby was born that changed the course of history. At the age of thirty-three He was hung on a cross. Even though Jesus fulfilled many foretold scriptures, healed the sick, and raised the dead, the Jews never understood what God was trying to do. Their Messiah, promised by God was literally under their noses, and the Jewish nation could not see Him. They had again missed the work of God.

Following the institution of the early church and the slaughter of many Christians at the hand of the Jewish religious leaders, the Jews again believed that they could serve themselves and over throw the Roman Empire. At that time, Rome sent leaders to crush the revolts once and for all. In 70 A.D., the Romans came in and burned the city of Jerusalem fulfilling Jesus' prophecy in Matthew 24:2 that not one stone of the temple would be left upon another. This was the final act of desolation for the Jews, and as time passed the Jews were dispersed throughout the world.

Due to this dispersion, the Jewish people lost their land, their name, their identity, and their language. No nation in the history of the world that had lost its culture, as the Jews did, had ever been able to recover. However, in 1948, the Jews were given back the land that they had lost. They quickly began to relearn their language and now, seemingly, have made a full recovery, with generations who have grown up with Hebrew as their native tongue. Even amid utter devastation, the plowman has overtaken the reaper. God kept his promises even after about 1875 years.

There are times when we may feel our lives are made up of bad decisions. We may even find ourselves reaping destruction as a consequence of the choices we have made. The Jews lost everything; they even sacrificed the Messiah, God's Son, but God kept the promises that He had made to them. He also has promises for us. Nothing can take us from the Master's hand.

PART 3
THE NATURE OF THE SPIRIT

Humans are amphibians—half spirit and half animal.
C. S. Lewis[17]

---

[17] C.S. Lewis, *The Screwtape Letters* (New York: Harper Collins, 1942, 1996) 37-38.

Chapter 10 – Spirit Versus the Flesh

In the last chapter we looked at knowing what we are going to reap. We discussed sowing to the flesh and how it reaps destruction, while sowing to righteousness (spiritual nature) reaps eternal life. In this chapter we are going to take a more in-depth look at the Spirit versus the flesh.

When the Spirit dwells inside of us, we cultivate a spiritual life. It does not happen all at once and may include times when we feel like failures. Nevertheless, it is a growing process and a time of cultivation. As we grow spiritually, we will notice more and more that we are leaving behind the characteristics of the flesh and taking on the characteristics of the Spirit.

What is the wrong with the flesh?

It is important for us to first begin by looking at the issue of carnality. Paul uses the Greek word *sarx*[18] which means flesh. This Greek word refers to the "soft substance of a living body" that covers the bones[19]. The flesh represents the basic nature of humanity, the primitive, animalistic nature. The flesh does not listen to reason; instead it is based entirely on

---

[18] Strong, 1996, G4561.

[19] Ibid.

satisfying personal needs. Animals do not logically think through their actions before they do them, they just do what comes naturally.

In the same way, the carnal nature is not controlled by reason since it focuses on satisfying our most primitive desires. For instance, people lie, cheat, steal, and even murder to ensure their own personal survival. Even though, over time, a person may continue to do these things out of habit or enjoyment, the initial purpose was to provide for a basic need or for self-preservation. Basically, serving our carnal desires satisfies our most primal need to survive.

When my kids were born, they spent the first year of their young lives selfishly wanting their basic needs met. They could not wait two minutes for the bottles to be prepared or to have their diapers changed. They wanted it right then. Babies live life in this basic primal nature. However, as they grow and are taught, they begin looking out for others, and over time they should develop a larger worldview. The older a child gets, the more tolerant he or she should become.

However, I have seen a lot of people in my life that never developed beyond that selfish, carnal nature. They may be forty or fifty years old but still wanting everything their way, immediately. Such people go into blind rages when the store does not have the type of ketchup they want, or their child spills milk on the carpet. I believe the reason that we see many date rapes lies in the fact that too many people are selfish and have never been able to move passed their carnal natures. The world is filled with people who are not able to control that natural animalistic nature because it takes effort to stop chasing our carnal desires, and no one can do it without the power of the Spirit.

Before we move on, we need to understand that none of these desires are wrong in and of themselves. Even though some people feel like certain desires, especially of a sexual nature, are impure, all God-given desires are normal. Nevertheless, allowing the desire to outweigh our reason and morals is wrong. For instance, a person will do whatever it takes to feed himself, because that is a natural need. However, instead of seeking assistance, some people will partake in an action that is immoral and even illegal. While the need for sustenance is primal and part of every living thing, the problem is in the method one uses to get it.

Romans 8:7 says, "...the carnal mind is enmity against God," which means anyone who follows the flesh is separated from God. In our fleshly nature we are enemies of God, fighting against the nature that God has for us. The nature that chases self-satisfaction wars against the nature of Christ, who gave up His rights, becoming obedient even to death on the cross.

What is so special about the Spirit?

Unlike many non-Christian religions as well as Christian denominations teach, true spirituality is not based on sacrifice but rather a truly consecrated life in Christ. Jesus did not ask us to die for him, but rather to live for him. Romans 8:5-6 says, "For they that are after the flesh do mind the things of the flesh; but they that are after the Spirit, the things of the Spirit. For to be carnally minded *is* death; but to be spiritually minded *is* life and peace." Remember earlier I said that we, in our basic nature, are at enmity with God? Christ is life, and if the flesh leads to death, then as death is separated from life, we are separated from Christ.

Sin separates us from God, and those who live their lives in sin are willfully rejecting Jesus Christ. The word "peace" refers to the bringing together of two opposing forces. The spiritually-minded are brought into fellowship with God. No longer are they at enmity with him, but now are at peace[20].

Unlike carnality that is based on selfishness, spirituality is based on selflessness. As we mentioned in the previous chapters, a tree that is not producing fruit is not allowing the nutrition to spread to the branches. A tree that is malnourished will have to expend its nutrients to maintain its trunk and branches first. If so, it may not produce fruit or may produce malnourished fruit. If a person is expending all his or her energy seeking after the things of the carnal nature, there will be no resources left to bear fruit.

To bear fruit we must be willing to make a selfless sacrifice. We cannot love unconditionally if we harbor hatred in our hearts. We cannot be temperate if we are self-indulgent. We cannot have peace at the same time that we are consumed with worry. Hatred, self-indulgence, and worry are all part of the fleshly nature. To truly be fruitful, we must move past the right to harbor these things in our lives.

What am I leaving behind?

When we live by the Spirit, the old nature has been done away with. In 2 Corinthians 5:17 it says, "Therefore if any man *be* in Christ, *he is* a new creature: old things are passed away; behold all things are become new." We have the ability to put fleshly desires behind us that used to rule our

---

[20] Radmacher, Earl D., Ronald Barclay Allen and H. Wayne House, *Nelson's New Illustrated Bible Commentary*, (Nashville: T. Nelson Publishers, 1999), Romans 8:6.

lives. Jesus said in John 8:34, "whosoever committeth sin is a slave to sin." Paul goes on to say, and I paraphrase, "Don't you know you are a slave to whomever you submit yourself." When sin had full reign in our lives, we were slaves to sin. That was the only way of life we knew. We may accept moral absolutes and try to live an "ethical life", but without Jesus permeating our hearts, none of our good works mean a thing.

As soon as we allow Jesus to come into the picture, we go from being a slave to sin, to a son of righteousness. In that moment the hold the old nature has on us is broken, and the new nature is borne. Jesus gave his life so that we could live. In return, our selfless sacrifice is the sacrifice of the flesh. In 1 Corinthians 15:31 Paul says, "I die daily." Daily, we have to make the conscious effort to overcome the sinful nature. Galatians 5:24 says that all who belong Christ have crucified the flesh. We are turning away from the carnal nature and developing the spiritual nature.

Furthermore, Romans 12:1 says, "that ye present your bodies a living sacrifice." The priests would take the lamb and slay it; spreading its blood for the sacrifice. A living sacrifice is not a dead sacrifice; instead Jesus paid the price for us so that we do not have to die for our sins. It is our reasonable service to live our lives by sacrificing the flesh. And this is how, "I am crucified with Christ: nevertheless, I live; yet not I, but Christ liveth in me: and the life which I now live in the flesh I live by the faith of the Son of God, who loved me, and gave himself for me."[21] It is no longer I who live but Christ who lives within me. Even though I still live in the sphere of the flesh I live by faith which allows Christ to live through me.

---

[21] Galatians 2:20

Spirit Versus the Flesh

This life is no longer ours; we were bought with a price, the precious blood of the Lord Jesus Christ. He came to give sight to the blind, bind up the broken, show love to the forsaken, and die so that we could have life. Only through his death, burial, and resurrection can we have the power to also overcome sin. John 10:10 says that Jesus died so that we could have life and have it more abundantly. As He reigns in our lives, the Holy Spirit gives us the power to walk in a right relationship with God.

How long does growth take?

Far too often, new Christians think that they will immediately overcome all obstacles in their way. A person accepts Christ on Sunday, but as soon as Monday morning hits, the desires of the flesh are back, and they lose faith. By Friday they are again sitting in the bar of the flesh becoming intoxicated on the disillusionment of the world. In our fast food, convenience store, "I want it my way, so give it to me now" society, we can begin to think that our walk with God will bring an immediate change in every aspect of our lives. We want to no longer desire sinful things; we want the addictions to disappear immediately; we want all the fear to wash away. When it lingers in the recesses of our hearts, we return to the same old problems.

For most people, giving up the carnal nature is a process. It takes time to move beyond our history of failures. You may still have struggles; we all do. Paul said, the good that I would like to do, I do not do, and the evil that I do not want to do, I do (paraphrased Romans 7:19).

Paul was a veteran in the faith who was raised as a Pharisee and ultimately became an Apostle of Jesus Christ. Nevertheless, he continued suffering with something that he wanted desperately to overcome. In 2

Corinthians 12:7-10 he refers to a "thorn in the flesh" that he continually suffered from. He stated that he asked God to remove it three times but relented when God revealed that "...[His] grace is sufficient" in our times of need. Likewise, you may have areas you want to overcome, but have yet to see the light at the end of the tunnel. Remember, that God's grace is always sufficient for us.

There was a woman minister that I worked with when I was in my early twenties. She was always working for the Kingdom of God, but she had some very serious problems. There were areas in her life that she was battling against, even up until the day she died. Even now, years later, I still consider her to be one of the greatest Christians I ever knew. It was not because she was perfect, but because she fought the good fight daily to overcome her flesh. In the same way, we also can fight daily through God's Spirit to build a deeper relationship with Him.

It is all about allowing the Spirit to work in our lives. The more the Spirit works, the more we will overcome. God has given us freedom and liberty in the Holy Spirit. We are not restricted by the Spirit; instead we are freed to live in the Spirit. Nevertheless, with that freedom comes the responsibility of putting the lusts of the carnal nature behind and pressing on toward the mark of the high calling in the Lord Jesus Christ.[22]

---

[22] Philippians 3:14

Chapter 11 – Gifts of Grace

This chapter is a little out of context in this book, but it is common for Christians to misunderstand the difference between the spiritual gifts and spiritual fruit. Without this understanding, confusion can set in causing individuals not only to ignore spiritual gifts, but even to deny their existence. For this reason, I am including this chapter to help differentiate between the two before we begin an in depth look at the fruits of the Spirit.

The fruits of the Spirit are basically the characteristics of the Spirit that indwell us, that grow, and develop over time. However, the gifts of the Spirit are much more diverse and can be manifested at any time. Also, the gifts may be different for different individuals. Paul gives multiple lists of Spiritual gifts, but it can easily be understood that God-given gifts extend much further than the ones on these lists. This chapter will help to provide a preliminary understanding of Spiritual giftedness.

What is a Gift

A Spiritual gift is one that's given according to the unmerited favor of God. It is a gift of grace. The word Charisma, which is translated "gifts" in the New Testament, comes from the Greek word *charis*, meaning "grace." God's gifts flow from his abundant grace. We do not deserve the gifts that God gives us; rather He chooses to provide these gifts liberally with the goal of our advancing the Kingdom.

First Corinthians 7:7 says, "But every man hath his proper gift of God, one after this manner and another after that." Everyone has a different gift depending on the grace of God. The verse in Romans 12:6 says, "Having then gifts differing according to the grace that is given to us..." We cannot do anything to deserve these gifts; they are given because of his love for us.

Following this statement in Romans 12, Paul provides a brief list of gifts. He says, "...whether prophecy, let us prophesy according to the proportion of faith, or ministry, let us wait on our ministering: or he that teacheth, on teaching...exhorteth, on exhortation...giveth, do it with simplicity...ruleth with diligence...showeth mercy with cheerfulness." Each of these is a gift bestowed by God, and it is to be exhibited in our lives according to the proportion of our faith.

In First Corinthians 12, Paul gives one of the most comprehensive lists of Spiritual Gifts. He lists the following gifts: word of wisdom, word of knowledge, faith, healings, working of miracles, prophecy, discerning of spirits, diverse kinds of tongues, and interpretation of tongues. Later in that chapter he adds apostles, teachers, helpers and administrators. Of these gifts, he states that even though these gifts are diverse, they were all given by the Spirit of God that enables the gifts inside of us.[23]

---

[23] 1 Corinthians 12:4.

Since Paul's lists are not exhaustive, I believe there are many other gifts not listed. I would also include talents such as abilities in art, music, and poetry, just to name a few. There are many other diverse gifts and talents exhibited in our world that God blessed humanity with. Every good and perfect gift comes from above.[24]

Why does God gift people who refuse to use the gift for Him?

Romans 11:29 says that the gifts and callings of God are without repentance. God chooses whom He will gift at His discretion, endowed by grace. God does not give gifts because He thinks the person deserves the gift, making the receipt of the gifts entirely unmerited. Therefore, if a person can do nothing to deserve the gift, then there is nothing that he or she can do to lose it.

Moreover, while the fruits of the Spirit are developed because the branches abide in the vine, gifts are not entirely contingent on the vine. Case in point, God has gifted many people with the ability to sing or write, but they do not all use it for Him. Like the prodigal son, people can choose to abuse and take advantage of the gifts of God. There are many truly gifted people in the world who have very strong callings and could advance God's Kingdom, but they choose to advance their own selfish kingdom. Nevertheless, there is always a gamble when God gives someone a gift or talent because that person has a choice of whom to follow.

---

[24] James 1:17.

What is the different between fruits and gifts?

Gifts of the Spirit differ from fruits of the Spirit in several ways, namely: purpose, manifestation, and function. Many times, they are used for edification, for ministry, and for spiritual warfare. On the other hand, the fruits of the Spirit are the basic characteristics of the Spirit, Himself.

Gifts are the Spirit are many times manifested suddenly in a moment of need while fruit are grown through spiritual maturation. Though people mature in their spiritual giftings, many times the gifts are innate or endowed through the reception of the Spirit. Some people are born with a musical talent or a Midas touch. On the contrary, the Spirit empowers us to develop fruits. Much like bodybuilding, developing fruits is the process of taking on the characteristics of the Spirit.

Functionally, the fruits of the Spirit are expressed on a personal level, and as the fruits grow in our lives, parts of our personalities begin to change. As we become more like God, our influence in the world becomes more profoundly affected by the fruits we are bearing. To say it more explicitly, the fruits of the spirit change us individually first before they affect the world.

On the other hand, the gifts of the spirit have several different functions, most of which act on a corporate level. Though some gifts, such as tongues, are for personal edification, other gifts, such as prophecy and tongues interpretation, are for corporate edification. Still other gifts are functional, such as leadership or administration. Nevertheless, each gift has a purpose and leaves a gap if it is missing.

What types of spiritual gifts exist?

Let us take a few minutes to look at the individual gifts of the Spirit as listed in the New Testament. There are eighteen different gifts mentioned, and they are found in Romans 12:6-8, 1 Corinthians 12:7-11, and 28-30, Ephesians 4:11, and 1 Peter 4:9-11. The *Baker Encyclopedia of the Bible* breaks these lists into four distinct groups based on the function of each gift: revelation, powerful works, leadership, and service.[25]

The first type of gift is called revelation. It is made up of divine inspiration that a person possesses that he or she would not normally possess. This area includes six diverse gifts: wisdom, knowledge, prophecy, discernment, speaking in other tongues, and interpreting tongues. These different gifts help to promote God's Kingdom through the spoken word.

The gift of wisdom is a divinely-inspired wisdom that someone possesses. As we age, we develop experiential wisdom because of the things that have happened in our lives. However, the gift of wisdom comes from God and is given for the edification of the Body of Christ. A person manifesting this gift can offer advice or have understanding that he or she would not naturally possess and is able to offer counsel regarding various aspects of life.[26]

The gift of knowledge works alongside the gift of wisdom. The gift of knowledge is divinely knowing about a person or situation, that he or

---

[25] Elwell, Walter A, and Barry J. Beitzel, *Baker Encyclopedia of the Bible*, Volume 2, (Baker Book House: Grand Rapids, 1988,) pp 1992-1995.

[26] Hayford, Jack W., and Herman Rosenberger, *Appointed to Leadership: God's Principles for Spiritual Leaders*, Spirit-Filled Life Kingdom Dynamics Study Guides, (Nashville: Thomas Nelson, 1994).

she would not normally have knowledge about.[27] It is usually a manifestation that reveals a specific need. However, it could also bring to light a sin or other problem that has not yet come to light. For instance, I know a pastor who confronted a person about pedophilia. Initially, the man refused help, until the police came knocking at his door.

Though many Christians equate the gift of prophecy with the ability to foretell the future, it is more accurately described as plainly speaking on behalf of God. Prophecy can be accomplished at a personal level through one-on-one edification, or it can also be exercised on the corporate level through preaching the Word. Throughout the Bible God revealed things to his prophets. Many of them gave warnings about the future, others offered judgment that was due because of the people's unwillingness to heed God's warnings, and others interpreted the promises of God for His people. These three areas are very similar to the message of preachers and pastors speaking on God's behalf though interpretation and the inspiration of God's Word.

The fourth gift is described as the ability to discern spirits, which is a spiritual awareness and intuition given by God. Much like a premonition, it allows the individual to recognize evil about a person or situation. It also helps a person to discern the spirit and motive behind an action. Typically, people with the gift of discernment can recognize things that others cannot recognize, and even have an impression of dread or sudden concern without knowing the reason behind it. Moreover, people with spiritual discernment are often able to recognize the works of Satan through

---

[27] Ibid.

demonic activities. Such individuals follow their instincts and later find out that they, or someone else, were almost victim to Satan's insidious plan.

Two of the most debated and potentially divisive gifts in the Bible are those of speaking in diverse tongues and the interpretation of tongues. Paul refers to praying in the Spirit as "the Spirit's way to pray for things for which we do not know how to pray."[28] It is praying the perfect will of God for personal edification. Since praying in the Spirit uses tongues that no one can understand, it is a form of communication directly through the Spirit. It is not meant to edify anyone else or to be used to speak to an assembly. Rather, it is our spirit's way of connecting with God and helps to rejuvenate our spiritual wellbeing.

Nevertheless, there are times when the gift of tongues is manifested in a corporate body to address a need or to bring edification. In 1 Corinthians 14, Paul talks about such an occurrence. When this happens there needs to be someone present who can interpret the tongues in order for the church to be edified. For this reason, many churches feel that tongues should be used in the corporate setting only if there is an interpreter present. However, just a few verses later Paul says in verse 39 and 40, "Be eager to prophesy, but don't forbid speaking in tongues, but be sure that everything is done properly and in order."[29] In this verse he explains that speaking in tongues for individual edification during worship is acceptable if it is not an address to the entire congregation.

---

[28] Romans 8:26.

[29] Tyndale House Publishers. *Holy Bible : New Living Translation*. 2nd ed. (Wheaton, IL: Tyndale House Publishers, 2004), 1 Corinthians 14:39-40.

These six giftings provide a way for spiritual edification for both an individual or on a corporate basis, by helping to provide insight into the mind of God and as inspiration for believers. While each has its own purpose, they are commonly used together to provide instruction. Furthermore, gifts in the revelation category can also supply a warning of natural and supernatural consequences of a person's, or a congregation's, actions. This could also help a people be aware of those who are trying to promote their own agendas.

The second type of gift is referred to as powerful works. This includes gifts that are powerfully demonstrated, such as faith, healing, and miracles. These gifts demonstrate the power of God as a witness to the world.

The gift of faith is different from the fruit of faithfulness that we will discuss in a later chapter. While the fruit of faithfulness grows and develops over time, the gift of faith is the ability to have a supernatural belief in God and His abilities. While everyone is given a measure of faith[30], some people are given a measure of faith that exceeds that of others. These people are endued with a special faith and can believe for anything: miracles, deliverance, etc.[31] Typically, they do not lose heart when the going gets tough. Instead, these believers have a supernatural trust in God and will see things come to pass.

---

[30] Romans 12:3.

[31] Hamon, Bill. *Seventy Reasons for Speaking in Tongues: Your Own Built in Spiritual Dynamo.* (Shippensburg, PA: Destiny Image Publishers, Inc., 2012), p 150.

Gifts of Grace

Next, is the gift of working miracles. A miracle is something that happens outside the normal realm of possibility. Throughout the Bible we read of many miracles: the virgin birth, the resurrection from the dead, the feeding the five thousand, and the parting of the Red Sea. Each of these events would have been impossible naturally. However, through the power of God, all things are possible.[32] God can make a way when we cannot see a way.

Furthermore, we also can see miracles in the aspect of healing. While healings can occur through several different means, miraculous healings are impossible without the manifestation of the power of God. Even with a doctor's help, a disease or illness does not suddenly go away. Nonetheless, we have all heard or even experienced a time when God has manifested His power and caused a tumor to dry up or a fever to suddenly cool. Whether God chooses to perform a miraculous healing or gives a medical professional the ability to complete a successful procedure, God takes care of his people.

The gifts of power are all supernatural in nature and provide a demonstration to the world. Much like Jesus explained to his disciples in John 9:3, miraculous works are done for the glory of God. There is no greater chance for a powerful witness than to see a genuine miracle. Therefore, when a person walks in the manifest power of God, he or she demonstrates God's work in the world.

<u>We will refer to the next type of spiritual gift as gifts of leadership.</u> These gifts assist with the ongoing needs of the church and provide

---

[32] Matthew 19:26.

leadership in ministry. The listed gifts of leadership include the gifts to become apostles, pastors, teachers, administrators, exhorters, and evangelists. Each different level has a distinct purpose but fills a different need of the church.

As Paul discusses areas of church leadership, apostleship is at the head of the list. Today's view of apostleship seems to be much different than the Biblical view of an apostle. Many churches that use the term "apostles" to ordain men and women as bishops or overseers in a group of churches. Even though apostles in the New Testament did take on overseer duties, they only oversaw churches they started. In a 2008 article by Skye Jethani, he describes the Biblical understanding of apostle as a minister who promotes the advancement of the Kingdom of God. He quotes William Beasley, who was a network leader with the Angelical Missions in the America's, as saying that the apostolic gift is a gift of, "…initiating new works to bring people to Christ."[33] In other words, the Biblical view of an apostle is one who is sent out to find new ways to reach the lost. Furthermore, many Biblical apostles took on the role as facilitator and overseer between the churches that he or she planted.[34]

The second area of leadership is that of pastoring and teaching. We group these together because God called those to whom this gift is given to be the leaders of the individual churches. They are the shepherds of the flock. Very rarely do you have a pastor that is not a teacher. Someone asked me recently why we felt that the pastor should determine what the people

---

[33] Jethani, Skye, "Apostles Today?", *Christianity Today*, (Spring, 2008).

[34] Ibid.

Gifts of Grace

need to hear instead of taking polls and teaching what the people want to hear. If the sheep knew what they needed, why would there be need for a shepherd? God anointed and ordained the pastor, who has been given the statutes of God. If the pastor was no different than the congregation, then there would be no need for the pastor. In 2 Timothy 4:3, it says that people have itching ears. They want to find ministers who will teach them what they want to hear, but rarely do we want to hear what we need to hear.

At the next level is the gift of governing and administration, allotted to those who are charged with the general overseeing of the church. This gift is given to individuals who allow God to use and bless their ruling and organizational abilities. There are some people who have a very special calling in business management, and they are ideal for administration over a church. God can use these abilities to help lead the business side of the church.

The role of exhortation can fall on any person. The purpose of the exhorter is to encourage people to move to a higher plain in the Kingdom of God. The church talks a lot about exhortation. The general idea is to build up or offer support and encouragement for one another. Paul exhorted those that he worked with. Throughout his epistles he continually encouraged and inspired them to move forward in their relationship with God and to seek out what God had for them. There are some people who have a special gift of encouragement and can inspire people to step out of their comfort zones. Such people are able to change negative situations into positive learning experiences to help others grow in their faith.

The last leadership gift is the gift of evangelism. An evangelistic gift is the desire to share the good news of Jesus Christ. The word evangelism comes from the Greek word *euangelion* which means Gospel or good news.

It describes those who have a passion or desire to share the good news of Christ with those they encounter. An evangelist is more than a person who just goes from church to church holding revivals. Rather. he or she is a person who is gifted in presenting the Gospel to the lost world. He or she may never preach a message or even lead someone in a sinner's prayer, but, instead, might demonstrate the love of God in such a way that draws others to the cross.

The final form of spiritual gifts is simply called the gifts of service. Like the gifts of leadership, the gifts of service are vital to the work of the church. A church cannot function without people serving in the non-leadership roles, and it cannot be left to the pastor to maintain it all.

First, the gift of helps belongs to those whose do not desire the spotlight or the middle of the action. These individuals are typically the background workers who help the leaders. They keep the ministry running smoothly while the leaders focus on the spiritual aspects of the ministry. The ministry of helps goes hand in hand with the gift of service, which is being willing to attend to the needs of others. Service-oriented people are typically the intercessors, the kitchen workers, the prayer support team, and other individuals whose goal is to help anyone that needs help.

The gift of giving can take on many different roles. The most common is monetary contribution. But there are some people who do not have the means to give large monetary donations but can give of their time through service. There are also those individuals who cannot give of their time but have the monetary means to make generous gifts to the church. Each person can give in his or her own way.

In Luke 21:1-4, we find Jesus sitting with his disciples, watching individuals bring their offerings to the temple. He saw the rich people celebrating their large gifts, but then he noticed a widow who had two small mites. While everyone else would have been pleased at the large sums of money that the wealthy offered, Jesus pointed out the two small coins the widow gave. He told his disciples, "This poor widow put in more than all the rest." As He explained, while the rich were giving only a portion of their wealth, the widow gave from the meagerness of her poverty. Some people are able to give a large amount of money, while others are able to give only a little. Nevertheless, both are important in the eyes of Jesus.

The final gift is that of mercy. Most Christians are quick to judge and lose faith in others. God gives to some a strong compassion and mercy for others. God shed his mercy on us. We would all be lost if it were not for Him; therefore, the least we can do is to show the same love and compassion for those around us. The gift of mercy allows us to love others by looking beyond their faults and becoming like Christ.

The Gifts of the Spirit are gifts that are given by the grace of God to the members of the body of Christ to bring edification of the Spirit and to promote growth church. In so doing, God gives us the honor of letting us partake in his ministry.

PART 4
THE FRUIT OF THE SPIRIT

Lord, make me an instrument of Thy peace;

--St. Francis of Assisi[35]

---

[35] Michael P. Green, ed., *Illustrations for Biblical Preaching: Over 1500 Sermon Illustrations Arranged by Topic and Indexed Exhaustively,* Revised edition of: The expositor's illustration file. (Grand Rapids: Baker Book House, 1989).

Chapter 12 – The Fruit of Love

What is love? Some people say that love is simply an emotion. Others say it is a chemical response in the brain to external stimuli. If we ask children what love is, and they will describe it by actions that demonstrate love. You ask teenagers, and they will describe it by the hormonal response that they are feeling. Even though love does not change, as we grow, our understanding of love does.

We just ended a chapter of the spiritual gifts of grace that God bestows upon us. In that chapter we spoke briefly about 1 Corinthians chapter 12. In chapter 12 of the first letter to the church at Corinth, Paul talks about the disparity of gifts among the individuals in the church. He ends the chapter by asking, "Are all apostles, are all prophets, are all teachers, are all workers of miracles? Do all have the gift of healing, do all speak in tongues, and do all interpret? But covet earnestly the best gifts." What gifts are better than these?

Notice he says covet the best gifts, but he does not tell us which one of these gifts are the best. Paul is implying that there are gifts that are more important, and they are not the gifts that most people would diligently

The Fruit of Love

seek. The greatest gifts are the ones that benefit others and build community.[36]

He concludes chapter twelve saying, "I will show you an even greater way." When the letters were written, the manuscripts did not have chapters and verses; instead it was written as one long letter. There would have been no division between chapters twelve and thirteen…like this.… "I will show you an even greater way; though I speak with the tongues of men and of angels and have not love, I become as a sounding brass or a tinkling cymbal…" The greatest gift of all, and the one that we should seek, is the gift of love.

I did not mention in the last chapter about love being a gift of the Spirit because it is not listed as a gift. However, judging from the way Paul ends chapter twelve and begins thirteen, I would dare say that love should be listed as a gift of the Spirit. It relates to the gift of service, helps, giving, and mercy. Love is different from all gifts and is actually the basis of all gifts. We will discuss this more in a later chapter, but first let us define love.

What is Love?

Musicians and authors have tried for centuries to describe love. It is mystical and poetic and can bring either joy or pain. No one can truly grasp the reality of love. In English we use the same word to say, "I love my mother," and "I love pizza." While, they are two totally different emotions, but we use the same word for both. The word love is used by

---

[36] Thiselton, Anthony C, *The First Epistle to the Corinthians : A Commentary on the Greek Text*, Electronic ed., (Grand Rapids: W.B. Eerdmans, 2000), p. 1167.

people to describe sexual desires, friendship, fondness, and compassion. For a foreigner coming to America, this can become very confusing. To solve this problem, the Greek language has several different words that mean love. The four most common Greek words for love are Eros, Phileo, Storge, and Agape.

<u>Eros</u>

Do you remember the little winged fellow that is on nearly every Valentine's Day card and is said to go around shooting people with arrows to make them fall in love? The Romans called this guy Cupid, while the Greeks called him Eros. He is the God of passionate sexual love. Eros is the root of the Greek word that is translated as erotic. It speaks of a passionate sexual attraction and desire to fulfill sensual needs.

Eros is not found in the New Testament; instead, it is found in secular writings. Since its use is sexual in nature and can refer to lust, it was not the word of choice for the Biblical writers.[37] Many ministers will refer to Eros as sinful, sexual lust, but Eros also describes sexual and intimate desire between a husband and a wife.

Marriages can be built on Eros love, but Eros can fade away over time. The strong sexual desire that a person has begins to wane as the excitement changes. If the relationship is built entirely on Eros, it will begin to fade away, leaving both individuals hurting and empty. Eros is a healthy kind of love that is built on passion and desire. It is filled with excitement,

---

[37] Spence-Jones, H. D. M, ed., *The Pulpit Commentary: 1 Corinthian*, (Bellingham, WA: Logos Research Systems, Inc, 2004), p.422.

The Fruit of Love

but it takes work to maintain Eros. Even in a marriage the partners must work to maintain their physical relationship. When it is neglected, the chance of infidelity rises.

Lust is the biggest problem with Eros. As we mentioned earlier, Eros was the Greek God of passion. He would strike his victims with flaming darts that would ignite their passions, especially lust.[38] Paul said, in Ephesians 6:16, "Above all, taking the shield of faith, wherewith you shall be able to quench all of the fiery darts of the evil one."

Lust is any intense, unbridled desire. It can be a desire for sex, affection, appreciation, possessions, or even power or protection. It can be a desire for possessions or material gain. Essentially, lust is the basis of all sin. While true love is self-sacrificing and based in the spiritual nature, eros is self-seeking and based in the carnal nature.

Phileo

The Greek word phileo talks of "spontaneous natural affection, with more feeling than reason."[39] Phileo describes affection and is used in such English words as Philadelphia, which is the city of Brotherly Love. Phileo is not based strictly on irrational physical attraction like Eros but is general affection.

We find this word throughout the New Testament. David Jeremiah, in his study on love, points out the conversation between Jesus and Simon in John 21 while they were sitting around the campfire eating. In the

---

[38] Keener, Craig S., *The IVP Bible Background Commentary : New Testament*, (Downers Grove, IL: InterVarsity Press, 1993), Ephesians 6:16.

[39] Elwell and Beitzel, 1988, p1357.

conversation Jesus asks Peter two times, "Do you love [agape – True love] me." Each time Peter replies, "You know I phileo you" or "you are my friend." The final time Jesus asks Peter, "Do you phileo me." David Jeremiah says that this change in verb emulates God's willingness to love us even when we are not ready to truly love him.[40] Jeremiah's idea is very encouraging to new Christians who are still working to develop true love.

No one knows the exact reason the evangelist used both words in this passage. It could simply have been the fact that during the New Testament phileo was commonly used interchangeably with the verb for true love. However, I tend to agree with David Jeremiah that the writer of the Gospel intended to show that Simon was not spiritually mature enough at the time to offer true unconditional love, since the general idea of phileo refers to an affection for another person.

Like Eros, Phileo can be lost. Friends can fall out of a friendship. People that at one time were close friends can move away and build new relationships. For this reason, phileo does not describe true, unconditional love.

Storge

Storge is a deeper love based on kinship, such as a parent to child, siblings, etc. This word is also used to describe a sexual relationship, but not fueled by passion, as eros, but rather a friendship that has deepened

---

[40] Jeremiah, David, *The Power of Love : Study Guide,* (Nashville: Thomas Nelson Publishers, 2004), p 10.

The Fruit of Love

into a sexual relationship. Such relationships are stronger than relationships built solely on Eros.

Storge is found in the New Testament, but only very rarely and in a compound form.[41] Even though storge is a love between family members, it is not the perfect unconditional, Godly love. Like the two previous types of love, family relationships can also be broken. Abuse and neglect can cause relationships to fracture. Misunderstandings and hurt feelings can divide even the closest connections. Therefore, storge does not represent the true characteristic of God.

Which type of love is true love?

We call the true Godly love "agape". It is not based on emotions and never changes. It is related more with moral principle than it is liking or affection.[42] Agape is committed love. I tell the youth that it is unconditional. Unlike Eros that is easily swayed by passion and desire, phileo that can be lost due to human imperfections, or storge which can be broken by distrust, abuse or betrayal, agape is unconditional. Nothing anyone can do will take away the agape form of love. In Romans, chapter 8, Paul says, "I am persuaded that neither death, nor life, nor angels, nor principalities, nor powers, nor things present, nor things to come, nor height, nor depth, nor any other creature shall be able to separate us from the love of God." Nothing we can do will cause God to love us any less.

---

[41] Elwell, Walter A., and Philip Wesley Comfort, *Tyndale Bible Dictionary*, (Wheaton, IL: Tyndale House Publishers, 2001), p 827.

[42] Elwell and Beitzel, p 1357.

True love is self-sacrificing. In John 15:13, Jesus says, "Greater love hath no man than this, that a man lay down his life for his friends." The greatest love focuses on other's needs instead of the needs of oneself. Jesus came and died on the cross not for His sake, but for ours. He loved us so much that He was willing to give His life for every one of us. Jesus died for everyone, even those who will never believe. Just because they are not saved does not mean that Jesus does not love them. Nothing can separate any of us, saved or unsaved, from the love of God, because God is love. He loves even the most lost sinners, and He wishes that they would come to know Him.

Jesus said, "A new commandment I give unto you, that ye love one another; As I have loved you, ye also love one another."[43] In this verse, Jesus calls us to have a deep-rooted love and compassion for others. Furthermore, agape is a love that is not contingent on our circumstances or situations. Instead, it is a love that is unconditional and never broken.

What is the difference between eros and agape?

Previously, we analyzed the differences between our carnal and spiritual natures. The carnal nature was self-satisfying, while the spiritual nature was self-sacrificing. Similarly, eros love is based in the flesh, while agape is based in the Spirit. Eros seeks out self-satisfaction. It desires pleasure and is based principally in lust. Agape, on the other hand, is based in moral love and compassion instead of passion and desire.

---

[43] John 13:34.

However, agape is not pious and cold as is seen in the lives of the Pharisees[44]. The Pharisees' demonstrated an eros kind of love. They would give so that people would believe they were righteous. Furthermore, they would stand on the street corner praying aloud so that all could hear, not as an honor to God but to stoke their own egos. Therefore, the Pharisees actions were not out of agape, but selfish desire. When the Pharisees demonstrated their righteousness as an act for all the world to see, they were not rewarded by God. Instead, Jesus said they received the reward they were seeking.[45]

Agape does not seek glory, but it seeks to glorify God. When we demonstrate agape, we are sharing the love of God with the world. When we abide in Him, we are growing the love of God. We love the world, so that the world will meet the wonderful savior. He loved them so much that He gave His only son. If He could sacrifice His son, why is it so hard for us to show love for others? Sadly, we may want to love others like God does, but our "selves" keep getting in the way.

How does Agape relate to God?

As was said a minute ago, God is Love. In 1 John 4:8, it says, "One who does not love, does not know God, because God is love." Agape love is the essence of God. Every time we love one another, we are spreading God throughout the world. We are showing God to the world.

If people want to know the characteristics of God, they can look at the characteristics of Love. In 1 Corinthians 13, Paul lists the characteristics

---

[44] Elwell and Comfort, 2001, p 827.

[45] Matthew 6:5.

of love. He says, "Love is patient, love is kind, it does not envy, does not boast, nor is it proud. Love is not rude, selfish, and it does not lash out in rage against someone else. It does not keep count of wrongs; it does not take pleasure in evil, but rejoices in the truth. Love patiently accepts all things, trusts all things, hopes all things, and endures all things. Love never fails." That plainly describes God. There needs to be no other explanation, God is love.

Chapter 13 – The Fruit of Joy

In the list of the fruits of the Spirit found in the book of Galatians, we find that joy is mentioned second. While joy may not seem as complex as love, it is just as vital to our spiritual health. What intrigues me about joy is that it is a way of life, and we can learn to have joy even when it seems that we should be miserable. Finding joy in the knowledge that we have a loving God that walks through every trial and tribulation alongside can help us reframe what we feel. Moreover, it can help to focus our energy on what we can change instead of fighting against what we cannot.

Is joy the same as happiness?

It is a very common misconception to equate joy with happiness. Happiness is an emotion that is based on a stimulus. For instance, something good happens, and we become happy about. Nevertheless, happiness is fickle and easily swayed. If something bad occurs, our mood can quickly waver from happiness to sadness.

On the other hand, joy is a mindset or a way of life. Instead of being swayed by our emotions, joy is finding contentment in all things that we have and do. The life that we live has its ups and down, but when we abide in a joyous realm, we are reminded that God is for us and He is always with us. There is nothing that life can serve us that God cannot overcome. There is no sorrow or trouble that is too big for our God to handle. Therefore, we can hold onto His hand, and he will sustain us through even the darkest of valleys.

Can I choose to be happy?

In the New Testament we learn many things about the Apostle Paul. The authorship of most of the New Testament books has been attributed to him, and he was one of the most prolific missionaries of his time. He planted more churches than the other Biblical missionaries, and he utilized every method of preaching the Gospel to reach the lost. In 1 Corinthians 9:22, he wrote, "I have become all things to all people, so that I might save one." In other words, he did whatever it took to reach the lost.

However, regardless of the triumphs of Paul's ministry, his life was not without sorrow. He went through more pain and suffering than most Christians will ever go through. Nonetheless, he pushed through his problems by holding tightly to the One in whom he believed.

In the book of Philippians, chapter 3, Paul provides his spiritual resume for the church at Philippi. He explains that he was a Jew who followed closely to the law. He was a Pharisee, one of the common Jewish leaders that opposed the work of Christ. The Pharisees gleaned all their theology from the Old Testament Law. While they believed in a literal resurrection after death, they also believed that the only path to God was through strict adherence to the Law. This is what led the Pharisees and other religious leaders to add numerous edicts to the God-given laws found in the first five books of the Bible. It was the Pharisees' diligence that finally forced Pilate to crucify Christ.

Not only was Paul a devout Pharisee, throughout his writings we also find that he was a Roman Citizen and held all the rights thereof. He was also a student of Greek philosophy and studied under a philosopher and doctor of the Law named Gamaliel. Holding this dual citizenship and his Greek training gave him many opportunities that other Christians did not have.

Paul had everything he needed to be one of the greatest Jewish religious leaders. He was so zealous for the Jewish faith that he even presided over the stoning of Stephen in an effort to eradicate Christianity. However, his whole way of believing experienced an about-face. While he was on his way to Damascus to continue his persecution of the Christians, he encountered God in the form of Jesus in a light so bright that it blinded him for three days.[46] By the time he regained his sight, God had removed the spiritual calluses from this heart.

After his life was changed, he no longer chased after the things of the Jewish culture, instead he chased after Christ with the same fervency that he had once pursued Judaism. In 2 Corinthians 11, Paul breaks it down for the church in Corinth. He explained how he was imprisoned many times and left for dead often. Five times he was whipped with thirty-nine lashes. He endured being beaten with rods three times. Three times he was shipwrecked, and once he was stoned. In addition to all these persecutions, he regularly faced problems from other Jews and Roman officials. Moreover, he was overcome with an intense desire to help those in the churches who were weak in their faith. If anyone had the right to be sad and upset, it would have been Paul.

---

[46] Acts 9:1-9.

Following Paul's third trek across Asia Minor to minister the Gospel to the many churches he helped to plant, he made his way back to the city of Jerusalem. He returned there so that he could bring a gift to the church at Jerusalem from the other churches in Asia Minor. When he arrived in Jerusalem, he was taken before the Jewish council and the high priest. He was also taken to the provincial governor. Paul would ultimately go to Rome by appealing to Caesar, but while he was in bonds in the prison under Festus, he had the opportunity to speak before the local ruler, King Agrippa II.

Acts 26:1 records that King Agrippa told Paul that he could speak on his own behalf instead of receiving a court-appointed advocate. This is the way Paul answered the charges against him, "I think myself happy, King Agrippa, because I shall answer for myself this day." In other words, he is saying I consider myself fortunate that I have the chance to speak on my own behalf. Paul had every reason to be upset, but, instead, he looked for the silver lining in the darkened clouds. He was content knowing that God was taking care of him.

That is true joy. He was not looking at all the problems. He was looking at the good that God was doing in his life. Not everyone would have the opportunity that Paul had to speak before the governor, nor was everyone allowed speak in Agrippa's court. But Paul did, and he was truly grateful for the favor God had shown him. Paul remained joyful even while enduring persecution because God was with him every step of the way.

The Fruit of Joy

How do I reap in joy?

Very few people read Psalms 126 unless they are going through some rough times in their lives. In this chapter the Psalmist refers to the captivity of Zion. As mentioned in chapter 4, the people of Jerusalem were captives in Babylon for seventy years. They were saddened at the loss of their home, their temple, and their way of life. In Psalms 126, a promise is written, "They that sow in tears shall reap in joy."

Those who continue to serve and work, even amid personal despair, will reap the harvest of God in joy. I need to be reminded of that sometimes. It is easy for a minister to get overwhelmed with the troubles of the ministry, and we are the ones who serve and build up the flock. If we can easily get discouraged, I can just imagine what it is like to be a member of the flock.

If we keep working and continue to sow even though it looks pointless, God will bring the harvest. Paul could have given up many times. He had a great life in the Jewish culture, but he had to start at square-one when he converted to Christianity. He had to make a very difficult decision. If he had remained in Judaism, we would not have most of the New Testament. Furthermore, Paul was a leader of the Gentile church; we can only imagine what it would have been like without him. He continued the work even when it looked hopeless, pushing back the walls of hell to advance the kingdom of God. Similarly, we need to maintain our joy in the midst of the toughest time of life.

Is it alright to have sad times?

When I was fourteen, I was ready to give up on everything. I felt that I had nothing to live for. I hated who I was, I was horribly hurt by some very important individuals in my life, and I did not want to live any more. The only thing I knew was that I loved to sing. I would spend hours in one of the spare bedrooms in our house practicing songs. I would stand there weeping and crying out before God.

Any time God touches me and gives me a word, I weep and weep. I can hardly talk sometimes because of the weeping. Recently we saw a movie called the *Holiday*, starring Cameron Diaz, Kate Winslet, Jude Law, and Jack Black. It is a good romance movie that my wife really liked. In the movie Cameron Diaz's character cannot cry while Jude Law's character cries about everything. That is me. I know the power of weeping.

Psychologists will tell you about the power of flushing out your problems through tears. Tears can release the great emotions that are locked deep within. The longer we leave our problems bottled up, the more miserable we get. When we finally let our emotions out, we can think more clearly and see the situation from a different perspective.

I learned at the age of fourteen that I had a very strong weapon against the enemy, and that was the power of letting out all my emotion before God and allowing him to take it all away. I am not saying that I have never let my emotions get bottled up, but I also know that I can lay my heart out before God, and He will be there to take all the junk and misery, and I can find pure joy in Him.

The Fruit of Joy

How can I overcome sadness?

We also find power in our praise and worship. Both acts show God our unending love for our Heavenly Father and are emotional releases for us. It is very difficult for some people to worship God. Macho men and others who have a problem showing their emotions have problems worshiping God because it is an emotional release. They are not willing to release their emotions.

In 2 Samuel 6, the people of Israel had reclaimed their most prized possession, the Ark of the Covenant. It represented the presence of God and was typically housed in the inner sanctum of the Tabernacle before the Temple was built under King Solomon. King David was overwhelmed with joy that the Ark was returning to its rightful place.

He took off his armor and weighted kingly garments and danced in the streets in a linen ephod. The linen ephod was typically a garment worn by the priests under their ornamental priestly breastplate. It could be speculated that David was essentially stating that the act of worship was more important than even the crown. Since David worshiped God in front of all the people of Jerusalem, this act of worship embarrassed his wife Michal who derided him for dishonoring his position and allowing the commoners to see him in a demeaning state.

He replied to her, "It was before the Lord…and I will yet be viler than this." In other words, he would do something more inappropriate and embarrassing than dance in his ephod, if that is what it took to give God praise. In response, God blessed David, but cursed Michal, causing her to be unable to bear children.

While it is humbling to release all our emotions before God; it is also liberating. The Word says that God inhabits the praises of his people.

We bless and glorify the Lord when we praise him, and in doing so we allow him full rein in us. Praise and worship bring joy into our lives.

How can I be joyful even in the bad times?

Looking back at the life of the Apostle Paul, we discover that Paul was also a worshiper. In Acts 16, we find Paul and Silas in jail. At midnight they were singing praises to the Lord, and a miracle happened. A great earthquake shook the jail and set them free. They could have easily been sitting in the cell, bitter and angry, thinking, "Why would God do this to us?" Instead they were rejoicing before the Lord.

Paul had grown into a place of contentment. In Philippians 4, Paul expounds on his understanding of true joy and being content. In Philippians 4:11, Paul wrote, "…for I have learned in whosoever state I am, therewith to be content." In verses 12 and 13, Paul speaks of suffering lack and enjoying abundance, but in either case, he learned that he could do all things through Christ Jesus. Then in verse 19, he declared in joy that God was willing and able to supply every need that he had.

Contentment is difficult for many people because people are seldom satisfied with what they have. They are worried about making more money or doing greater things. I have had people ridicule my choices to be a minister, teacher, and author instead of finding a "real job" and making a lot of money. It is not all about money. The greater good is changing the lives of others and helping them to understand the gift of God, which is salvation.

Paul reminds us time and time again to be content. Interestingly, he never said that he had gained contentment, instead he said he had learned

The Fruit of Joy

to be content. Being content is a learned process, and no one ever fully masters it. It is something that we develop, like a fruit, and it grows in our lives. We must choose to be content. The more we learn to be joyful even when we feel we have nothing to be joyful about, the more we will discover that we are richly blessed. When the seed of contentment is planted, it grows joy. The more the seed grows, the stronger our joy becomes.

As in the growth of any other seed, learning to be content takes time. We begin by choosing to have a positive attitude when we would normally have a negative one. Also, we begin to find the good in things around us. As we learn to overcome sorrow and fear, we become adept at joyous living, no matter what state we are in.

Why should I be thankful in suffering?

Consequently, as we grow in our ability to experience joy, we also grow in our ability to give thanks. This idea goes back to our discussion on praise and worship. Just as Paul was content in all things, he looked for things he could be thankful for. Instead of looking at his persecution, he was thankful and felt fortunate that he was allowed to speak before King Agrippa. He looked at the entire situation and had every chance in the world to be bitter; instead, he made the conscious effort to be happy and gracious.

He said, "I think myself happy," or "I feel very fortunate." He was focusing on the good things. He was focusing on the things that he could be thankful for. Naturally, humans choose to be miserable. If there is not some chemical imbalance or psychological disorder, a person is miserable by choice. And misery loves company. If I am miserable, I want to talk about my problems and make everyone else miserable, too.

I was in a restaurant a short time ago and heard a gentleman behind the counter griping and complaining because he was sick. He was talking out loud to himself saying, "I should have just stayed home; I am so tired." My first reaction was to reach behind the counter and slap him upside the head, but I refrained. I thought, "What is his attitude saying about his place of business?" What is your attitude saying about you?

Our outlook on life tells something about who we are spiritually. If we are focusing on the problems in life, we are not content and therefore do not have joy. If we look for the positive things of life, we choose to be thankful and content. Happiness comes from true joy and contentment in all things. It can only come from learning to be thankful and trusting God no matter what is going on in our lives.

Chapter 14 – The Fruit of Peace

While every year more and more diseases fight against the health of humanity, the most common ailment in the hustle-bustle world in which we live is worry. Since Valium arrived in the early 1960's, prescriptions for anti-anxiety medications have soared. Worry and anxiety plague millions of people every day. There are times that I am hit with overwhelming feelings of anxiety. Even after years of struggling to overcome my anxious personality, sometimes I feel that I am going backward instead of forward. For me, most of my worry and anxiety are due to my biological makeup, as well as things that have happened throughout my life. For those readers who are treating their anxiety and depression with medication, this chapter is in no way recommending discontinuation of medication. Nevertheless, for people who are overwhelmed with worry, I have your best antidote…peace.

In this chapter, I am going to try to present something to you that you can start doing to help you find greater peace in your life. I sometimes read a book expecting it to help me with areas of my life but end up dissatisfied. It may give a lot of great information and encouragement, but it does not tell me what I can do differently. I will try not to do that.

Out of the eighty times "fear not" is used in the Bible, well over sixty of those times someone is telling someone else not to fear. In many of the cases God is saying it, while other times God's spokesmen are saying it. What comforting words… "fear not". Imagine sitting with the shepherds on the grassy plain one warm Bethlehem night, and all of a sudden a light breaks through the darkness and an Angel is standing before the shepherds. The shepherds had never seen an angel before, but that night was no ordinary night. Then the angel opened his mouth and said, "Fear Not."

Seeing the Heavenly hosts would have stricken anyone's heart with fear. It would have startled even the most devout follower, so you can only imagine how the shepherds felt. They were not learned men and probably had heard of God only on the Sabbath. Nevertheless, the angels bore Good News which filled the Shepherds' hearts with peace.

Moreover, fear is a very common part of life. We all deal with it in one aspect or another. For instance, my boys are the greatest kids I could ever have hoped to have. However, they love to wait until about 3:00 in the morning when I am sound asleep to start screaming because there is a shadow on the wall and they became fearful. My wife handles this with great finesse; she sleeps right through it. I, on the other hand, trudge my way through the house trying to figure out what is going on. I make it to the room and find both boys sound asleep. Even though I go back to bed, I am now wide awake.

I have had to tell them many times, "There is no such thing as monsters," but childhood imagination prevails. I remember my own imagination as a child. I used to use old boxes and chairs to build time machines and rockets to the moon. I remember one time I oversaw two other kids while they built a dog house for my stuffed dog named Little Beggar.

Active imaginations can be very beneficial; they spawn ideas and lead to innovation. Nevertheless, when the lights are out, and you are alone in your room, that imagination can keep you awake all night long thinking about the shadows in the closet or the monsters under the bed. You do not want to put your feet down for fear of being grabbed, and nighttime television does not help.

Worry can be caused by an over-active imagination. We always worry about the far negative end of the spectrum. Most people who get a weird pain immediately look it up in the medical guide on online to find out what major disease they have. Or when the boss says, "I need to talk to you in my office", most of us do not think, "I am getting a raise." The first inclination is to wonder, "What did I do wrong?" We imagine the most negative consequence first.

How does worry affect me?

Worry has not only been linked to many physical illnesses, it has also been linked to spiritual illnesses. If we are being controlled by worry, we cannot truly have faith in God. If God is God, He will take care of us. We must allow Him to be God. Worry's premise says, "I have to do something to take care of this," which essentially says, "God, I cannot trust you to take care of this matter." In other words, we are saying that we are more powerful than God or that He is not trustworthy to handle the situation. If we cannot trust Him, then He is not God over our lives.

Worry comes from fear. If we fear something, it manifests itself as worry or anxiety inside of us. As peace grows in our spirits, we see the worry and fear begin to dissipate. Worry is the byproduct of fear; peace is the byproduct of faith. It is our reaction to the inner assurance that we can truly rely on God, whatever the situation or how hard life gets.

In Proverb 3:5-6, we read, "Trust in the Lord with all thine heart; and lean not unto thine own understanding. In all thy ways acknowledge him, and he shall direct thy paths." The phrase "Direct your path" can also be translated, "make your path straight." We were discussing this in Bible Study one night, and the question was asked, "What does it mean make your paths straight?" Think for a minute about a winding tunnel, like the catacombs. They twist and turn, and many forks lead to dead ends. We can get lost and wander through them for hours.

Now think of a tunnel that is straight. From one end you can see out the other end. Much in the same way the path of life is filled with curves and turns, and we cannot see the end goal, but God places the end goal in focus. He does not remove the obstacles and the problems; He just aligns us so that we can be focused upon the goal.

Even amid turmoil we can have peace. If we submit our ways to Him, we can believe that He will take care of us. Consider Simon Peter in Matthew 14:22-36. Jesus sent his disciples to cross the sea of Galilee while he sent away the crowds. In the middle of the night, a storm came upon the water. Jesus came walking across the water towards the boat that the disciples were in. Initially, the disciples were frightened, but Simon called to Jesus, "Lord, if it is you, tell me to come to you on the water."

Seeing his faith, Jesus instructed Peter to walk on the water. It was an awesome miracle, until Simon Peter took his eyes off the Lord and focused on the waves. Suddenly, he was sinking like a lead weight. Jesus saved him from drowning. I suppose that later in Peter's life he remembered this and the many other memories where Jesus delivered him, while penning the words in 1 Peter 5:7, "Casting all of your cares on Him for He careth for you."

How can I overcome worry?

In the book of Second Kings, chapter 6, we read an incredible story about the prophet Elisha. We see the man of God surrounded by hostile soldiers and chariots. Engaging in hand-to-hand combat with a charioteer would be like trying to sword fight a moving car. It can be done, but the chariot driver would have an overwhelming advantage. Elisha's servant looked and saw the multitude that was warring against them, and he began to tremble in fear. Acknowledging the servant's fear, Elisha said, "Fear not."

Picture this with me for a moment, there is an entire army out to get them, and Elisha says, "Fear not." His servant had to wonder, "What is going on in his head? Fear not? Is he crazy? We are surrounded by enemy soldiers, and he says 'fear not'!"

Nevertheless, Elisha knew something his servant did not. He continued, "For they that be with us are more than they that be with them." Then he prayed, and God opened the servant's spiritual eyes. He could see the spiritual army that stood around them. The mountain was full of horses and chariots of fire sent from Heaven by the Lord.

It is a fact that the army of God is greater than the army of the world. I have dealt heavily with this issue. I was raised in a fearful household. My family tends to exaggerate, so I came by it rightly. It is easy for me to feel as if I am under attack. It is not that I reject correction, because I know that correction is the only way to grow. But if the correction is handled in a confrontational way, I begin to panic and shut down. Partly due to environmental issues and to a condition called attention deficit disorder, I allow what I perceive that people think of me to cut deep wounds that others struggle to understand.

God did not call us to be overwhelmed by distress, but to live in peace even when we are distressed. Jesus never said that life would be easy. In John 14:27 He says, "Peace I leave with you, my peace I give unto you: not as the world giveth, give I unto you. Let not your heart be troubled, neither let it be afraid." This peace gives us the strength to walk on even when we are struggling. He did not say, "Follow me and I will make the road easy," instead He said, "take on my yoke." In our weakness His strength is made perfect. When Jesus says, "take my yoke", he means share yokes with me, let me carry one side and you the other.

In Romans 8:28, Paul wrote, "God will work all things for the good of those who believe and are called according to His purpose." Even though many people try to interpret this verse to say that life would be perfect, it does not; it states that God can take anything, good or bad, and make things turn out alright.

Then, not even three verses later, Paul makes another profound statement. He says, "If God be for us, who can be against us?" In other words, if the all-powerful, all knowing God is fighting on our side, then why do we try to add to God's work by worrying and fretting about the world in which we live? Who can add one moment to his or her life by

The Fruit of Peace

worrying?[47] No matter how much we think about the future or the past, or even what we will eat or wear, no amount of worrying will add to our days. Nevertheless, Proverbs 3:2 says that it is by keeping His commands that we will add days to our life and peace to our days.

How do I maintain peace when I am troubled?

In Exodus 14:14, we read, "The lord will fight for you and ye shall hold your peace." Shortly before this verse, Moses had led the children of Israel out of Egypt. The Egyptians were in hot pursuit. The children of Israel did what they were good at doing; they began complaining.

They said to Moses, "What? Because there were no graves in Egypt you brought us to the wilderness to die?"

The Red Sea was before them, and the Egyptians were behind. Fear was their first reaction. There was no logical answer. Their finite reasoning said they were going to die, because every foreseeable outcome was death.

In Exodus 14, Moses essentially said, "The Lord will do your fighting, so shut up." Maybe he did not say it that way, but that was what he meant. God will do the fighting for us. We can complain and worry forever, but it will never change the situation.

Much later, when David was standing in front of the Philistines, he had every reason to be worried. He had neither armor nor weapon. All he had was a sling and five smooth stones. But he knew in whom he had believed, and he said in 1 Samuel 17:47, "And all this assembly shall know that the Lord saveth not with sword and spear: for the battle is the Lord's, and he will give you into our hands." It is not our battle. No matter what

---

[47] Matthew 6:27

we say and do, it is not our battle. Since God put you here, He is the One that has to take care of you. It is His battle. Let Him do His job.

In Matthew 10:28, Jesus said, "Fear not them which can kill the body but cannot kill the soul, but rather fear him which is able to destroy both body and soul in hell." Do not worry and be afraid of people and their thoughts of you, because God is the only one that matters. As long as our hearts are true to God, He will give us favor with those around us.

What if I feel I have failed God?

As mentioned before, in the flesh we are at enmity with God, but the blood of Jesus Christ brought us into alignment with Him. The widening chasm between God and man continued growing because of sin, but the blood of Jesus filled the gap and bought us the ability to be at peace with God. When we are at peace with God, there is no reason to worry.

Nonetheless, the devil torments us. He reminds us of our past in an effort to destroy our future. There is no "wham bam" healing that will cause us to never worry or fear again. There is no medicine that will remove all chance of anxiety and fear. Though it is impossible in the natural world, with God all things are possible.

In 1 Corinthians 10:3-7, we are told that we do not war against the flesh; instead, we are told to tear down strongholds. In verse 5 we discover that the means of tearing down strongholds is by, "Casting down imaginations and every high thing that exalteth itself against the knowledge of God and bringing into captivity every thought to the obedience of Christ..." In other words, as we bring every thought into captivity, we can overcome the irrational feelings that we have.

The Fruit of Peace

We need not let any thought go through our minds without thoroughly examining it. If we keep thinking the same way we have always thought, we will keep feeling the way we have always felt. Psychologists have a technique for overcoming irrational thoughts. It is called self-talk. Essentially, when the negative or harmful thought enters the mind, the person recognizes it and immediately rejects it by verbalizing. Some people verbalize the opposite of the irrational thought; others verbally reject the thought.

I use self-talk throughout the day to overcome negative thoughts and attitudes that run through my mind. I often tend to feel guilty, embarrassed, frustrated, and anxious when I think about negative things… especially when I remember things that I have done wrong. The same old feelings saturate me. God has helped me recognize them, and most of the time I can stop the thought by verbalizing, "I am not thinking about that." My kids look at me weird, but for me the verbalization helps to stop the thought in its tracks.

If you want peace, then make the effort to change how you think and react. "Finally, brethren, whatsoever things are true, whatsoever things are honest, whatsoever things are just, whatsoever things are pure, whatsoever things are lovely, whatsoever things are of good report; if there be any virtue, and if there be any praise, think on these things."[48]

Can I really have peace in the middle of chaos?

Putting aside all vain imaginations and focusing on God is the most important thing that we can do as Christians. If we allow ourselves to be

---

[48] Philippians 4:8

swayed by every fear and heartache, how will we ever see the maturity of peace in our lives? But if we focus on God, we will find that even in the midst of despairing circumstances we will have hope.

A few years ago, I was talking to a friend of mine about peace. There had been an area in my life where I was getting caught up in despair. I was letting fear rule my life. I continued to seek God about the situation, and finally it changed. I was filled with peace. While talking to this friend, he said, "But is it real peace? Real peace is not based on the situation but based on knowing that God is in control." Slap…I was so happy that I had made it to a place where I felt that the burden had been lifted, and now He was throwing a kink into my perfect little world. Actually, I fully understood his statement. It is refreshing to have that time of peace after a storm, but there is a peace that is much higher. It is the peace that passes all understanding.

Philippians 4:7 says, "And the peace of God, which passes all understanding, will keep your hearts and minds in Jesus Christ." It is easy to have peace when the storm is over, but what about having peace in the midst of the storm? When Jesus and the disciples were on the boat and the storm came up, the disciples panicked, but Jesus was at peace. He was not worried about what was happening outside. While the boat tossed and pitched, He was asleep. He slept through the storm.

I cannot wait until my boys begin sleeping through the storms. We have thunderstorms that will pop up in the middle of the night as the warm air begins to cool. As soon as the first thunder rolls, my oldest will be at the foot of my bed. We have a spot now that is designated for them to sleep on the floor. It is a place where they can feel secure even in the midst of the storm.

There is a peace on which we can rely, also. It is a peace that only God can give. This peace also breeds peace in others. When we are truly at peace, others will look at us and think, "I would like to find a peace like that." As we plant peace in our lives, it will grow and blossom into the most beautiful flowers. It is a peace that the world cannot comprehend, yet people will want the same kind of peace.

Chapter 15 – The Fruit of Patience

Several years into my ministry as a Pastor, I decided to take the church through the book of Romans. We studied Romans every Wednesday night for two full years. In the study we went through every line and every premise in the book of Romans. Sometimes we read only a verse a night; other times we got through a passage a night, and sometimes we dwelt on just a word. Nevertheless, we went through the entire book from start to finish. It was a very long process, and even though I love exegetical Bible Study, I could not wait until it was over.

Taking two years to go through one book of the Bible can be very enlightening. I learned things that I would never have expected to learn. I also was bored out of my mind at times. Sometimes Paul goes on page after page, chapter after chapter, repeating the same thing over and over. Through the study I learned a lot about patience, both from the research and the monotony.

What is Patience?

It will be good for us to begin looking at patience by asking the question, "What is it?" One of the best places to find the definition of patience is in Romans, chapter 15. In verses 4-5 we read, "For whatsoever

The Fruit of Patience

things were written aforetime were written for our learning, that we through patience and comfort of the scriptures might have hope. Now the God of patience and consolation grant you to be likeminded one toward another according to Christ Jesus."

In these two verses we find the word "patience" a couple of times. First, Paul says that by the things we find in the Word that were written before us, we can find patience and comfort. The word "patience" can also be translated as perseverance.[49] To persevere is to be steadfast and endure, to weather everything that comes our way. The word, "persevere," means to maintain motivation and stride even when it may seem impossible.

The word translated as "comfort" is the word *paraklēsis* which is related to the word *paraklete*, which means encourager or advocate. The Holy Spirit is called the *paraklete*, or a comforter and counselor. He works on our behalf to help us in our time of need, encouraging and admonishing us to keep going.

From Paul's statement we discover that God, through His work and His word, drives us to endure and persevere by giving us the strength to keep going when our strength is gone. And He encourages us along the way. God is like a coach. A good coach pushes his or her team for excellence. The coach is the one responsible for keeping the team motivated even when no hope remains. He or she is the trainer and worker whose goal is success, and when the team is put to the test, the coach is the one who runs along beside them yelling, "Come on you can do it!"

Think of a person running a long race. Deep into the race, nearing the finish line, his body becomes weak, his legs are like jelly, and he feels he

---

[49] Strongs, G5281.

cannot go one step farther. Then he hears the words of the coach encouraging him and pushing him to finish. That is the same way God helps us to make it to the end.

How can I have real contentment?

Let us take a moment to revisit Paul's words regarding contentment that we examined in the chapter 13. In Philippians 4:11, Paul makes a very profound statement. He says, "I have learned no matter what state I am in, to be content." Even if his life was in jeopardy, he was determined to be content. No matter if he was on the edge of darkness, he was content.

As we stated previously, nearly every negative or discouraging or painful thing that could happen to a person happened to Paul. Nevertheless, he was content in all things. There was so much that he could have been troubled about. Paul could have been filled with anxiety and depression. He could have hated God and those who persecuted him so relentlessly. But no matter what circumstances he was in, he was content.

How then can one be content? It is a change of the mindset. Before we accept Christ, we spend most of our lives absorbed in the ways of the world. People can easily become overwhelmed by the choices offered by the world, like money, fame, fancy houses, clothes, etc. Nevertheless, we can begin to change our mindset by making a choice to trust God. When we give it to Him, He will take care of it for us. We cannot lay down our burden at church on a Sunday morning just to pick it up on the way back out the door. That defeats the meaning of what Jesus told us to do in Matthew 11:28, "Come unto me, all ye that labour and are heavy laden, and I will give you rest."

The Fruit of Patience

There is a fork in the road of everyone's life. We can either continue down the road, focusing on the world and its values, or we can refocus, shifting our hearts toward God. To truely grow contentment, we must change the way we look at life. For instance, I hear parents complain that they spend their entire paychecks on bills, food, clothes, and kids' activities, leaving little room for anything else. While this may be the fact, it is the wrong way to look at the situation. We should be rejoicing that we have the wherewithal to pay our bills and a family to share our love with.

There are many people, rich in the eyes of the world, who would give everything they own to have the real love of a family. There are many families whose bank accounts are empty because of a devastating illness of a child. There are always others who have it worse that we have it, so we need to learn to be content with what He gives us and where He puts us and wait upon the Lord.

What does contentment have to do with patience?

Continuing with that same thought, let us flip over for a moment to the book of Romans, chapter 5. We start reading in verse three. It says, "…glory in tribulations also, knowing that tribulation works patience; and patience, experience; and experience, hope." Why would we glory because we are in the midst of tribulation? That's not what it says. Paul tells us to glorify God in spite of tribulation.

Tribulation refers to pressure, pressing together, and distress. We think of trials, abuse, persecution, but tribulation is the act of grinding two things together and breaking them down. Have you ever been stressed? That is a form of tribulation. It is any type of pressure that works to break us down. We glory not in the fact that we are going through tribulation, but rather that He is God even in the midst of tribulation and stress.

We can actually walk through life rejoicing and glorifying God, even in the midst of despair. If we do, it will build character in our lives. Life builds character and brings patience, which leads to experience. Everyone would like the testimony without the test. Everyone would like have the benefits of the experience without having to actually experience it.

Recently I was talking with a parishioner about the stress that he and his wife were under. They had this false hope that God would just miraculously intercede and "zap", everything would be perfect. I had to let them in on a little secret. It does not work like that. Life still has trouble and we have to trust God through it.

God works in those types of situations in two different ways. His first option is to stand up on the bow of the ship and yell to the waves, "Peace, be still," and the wind and waves abate. His second and more common option is to walk on the water, get in the boat, and help us ride out the storm.

We all want the "Peace, be still" moment, but most of the time He rides the waves with us. God does not cause tribulations, or stress, but He does use it. In Romans 8:28, it does not say He will ease all of the pain that a person goes through. It also does not say that He will cause us pain so that He can teach us. It says, "And we know that all things work together for good to them that love God, to them who are the called according to His purpose."

Have you ever read the verses immediately preceding verse 28? Verse 26 says that the Holy Spirit prays for us when we do not know what to pray. Verse 27 says that these intercessions are made according to the perfect will of God. Then we get to verse 28, which says that through the acts of the Holy Spirit in our lives, God will take all the junk that comes against us and work it out for our good.

The Holy Spirit is there to work on our behalf and will even intercede for us when we are unable to intercede for ourselves. Unlike our mortal prayers, the words of the Holy Spirit line directly up with the will of God. That way, as He is working on our behalf by working out all of the pain and hurt that we have gone through and using it to make us stronger.

Many Christians believe that God sends bad things upon us to teach us something. Many also believe that God tests us just to teach us. Instead, as with Job, the devil is the one that brings on the trials and does the tempting. God is not going to send temptation. It would be like me telling my son, "Stay out of the street," and then putting his favorite toy in the middle of the yellow line. God is not like that. In James 1:13-16, it says, "Let no man say when he is tempted, I am tempted of God: for God cannot be tempted with evil, neither tempteth he any man: But every man is tempted, when he is drawn away of his own lust, and enticed. Then when lust hath conceived, it bringeth forth sin: and sin, when it is finished, bringeth forth death. Do not err, my beloved brethren."

Through the work of the Holy Spirit in our lives, God is able to take the things that we go through… tribulation, temptation, and pain…and teach us how to get through it. Tribulation bears patience which also bears trust in God. The next time we feel things going downhill, we shouldn't immediately begin complaining about the problems that we are going through. Instead, we should rejoice in God's love and provision in spite of our suffering, and then we will be able to see the spiritual fruit that is born in our lives as He helps us work through it.

Chapter 16 – The Fruit of Gentleness

Describe being gentle. When I hear the word gentle, I think of taking care of a baby or something fragile. I see the sign, "Handle with care" or "Fragile". Gentleness almost sounds out of place among the other fruits of the Spirit. The Spirit of God invokes boldness to minister and witness the Good News. What does that have to do with gentleness?

How do we define gentleness?

The word "gentleness" means "benign". That definition did not help me out, either. When I hear benign, I think of a type of tumor. Instead, "benign" literally means harmless or causing no harm. Therefore, gentleness means to "cause no harm".

My mom used to tell me I was like a bull in a china closet because I would come running through the house being loud and destructive. I did not think it was that bad until I had a son that definitely took after his own father. Our youngest son is on the Autism Spectrum. His definition of gentle is not popping the kitty's head off when he pets it.

My children are not gentle. They all have their scrapes and bruises. My princess is like "Xena, the warrior princess" in her lacy dresses and big poufy bows, yielding a broom as her battle sword against her brothers. My wife looks at me and says, "They are why we cannot have nice things."

We are all human, and we have human impulses. How easy is it to get angry and take that anger out on those around us? How easy is it to get caught up in the heat of the moment and say something that we wish later we could take back? That is human nature. We suffer from a sickness called "The Fall," and many times when that ugly head of the flesh comes up, we act in ways we never intended to act.

Nevertheless, as we put aside the human nature, allowing God to rule our lives, our personalities change. Instead of being quick to anger, spouting off things in a knee-jerk reaction, we begin to approach things differently. It is easy to respond hastily to others' actions, and it is hard to refrain from responding even when we are sure that the other person is in the wrong. But the Spirit calls us to be gentle**,** or benign.

How do I overcome wrath?

Proverbs 15:8 says, "A wrathful man stirs up strife, but he that is slow to anger appeases strife." He who is wrathful worsens the situation, but he who slows down and takes time to weigh the situation will help to resolve it.

This gentle attitude is an intrinsic characteristic of God. Psalms 145:8 says, "The Lord is gracious and compassionate, slow to anger and plenteous in love." God does not jump to conclusions, and He does not react out of emotion. Instead, He is compassionate and takes His time. If only we could be slow to anger. Every year people are jailed because they were driving on the highway, and when someone cut in front of them, they become furious and react accordingly.

I recently heard a story of a husband and wife who were driving down the highway. Some guy cut them off, and the husband started rolling down the window yelling threats and shaking his fist. His wife, horrified, said, "Honey stop that, we're driving the church van." Have you been there?

Allowing ourselves to act out of rage and anger can do extreme damage, and nothing good comes out of it. Instead, we are called to take on the characteristics of the Spirit by not allowing the flesh to overtake our rationality. For this reason, it is important to remember that sowing to the flesh reaps corruption but sowing to the Spirit reaps eternal life.[50] As we allow the Spirit to infiltrate our hearts, the rough edges of our hearts begin to soften.

How do I soften over time?

The proper word to describe the softening process of the Spirit is "mellowing." This means ripening and becoming seasoned over time. It refers to a maturing and rounding off of something that has the potential to be severe and harsh. It is the desire to show grace even when we have the right and option to be angry.[51] We see this idea of mellowing in several places in the Bible, one of which is Jesus' statements in the book of Luke about a person partaking of old wine. He says that one who drinks old wine will not immediately desire new wine. Because the old wine is better and has mellowed with age.

---

[50] Galatians 6:8

[51] Friberg, p.410.

Like wine, tea also mellows with age. White, green, and black tea all come from the same leaves. White tea is the healthiest with many antioxidants and the mildest flavor because it comes from very young tea leaves. Green tea comes from older leaves, is a little stronger, but still has antioxidants. Black tea, being the strongest, is from even older leaves. The taste and strength of the leaf changes as it matures.

The mellowing-out process is not hurried. It happens over time and through growth. Various times in this text we have looked at the lives of the Biblical writers. Think with me back to Simon Peter. Who was he when he first met Jesus? He was a fisherman whose main concern was making a living. In the synoptic Gospels, Peter even told Jesus, "We have left everything to follow you."

Later in His ministry when Jesus asked him, "Who do you think that I am?" Peter quickly answered, "The Christ." Not many days after that, as Jesus talked of his Christological duties of death, Peter rebuked him. Peter was full of zeal. At the last supper he promised Jesus that he would never forsake Him. In the Garden of Gethsemane, he even cut off a servant's ear in an attempt to protect Jesus. But when he sat with the servants around the campfire listening to Jesus' trial before the religious leaders, Peter cursed and denied knowing Jesus.

As we discussed earlier, Peter was the only disciple that stepped out of the boat to walk on the water. He was also the first to sink. However, after the infilling of the Holy Spirit on the day of Pentecost, Peter was the one to preach and lead 3000 people to their savior Jesus Christ.[52] There was

---

[52] Acts 2:41

The Fruit of Gentleness

a difference in Peter's personality after he was filled with the Spirit. He was no longer the middle-aged hotshot full of zeal and a bad temper. Now he took time to speak out of the love and the care of God. He was no longer worried and concerned about life. He knew that God had always provided, and He would provide until the end. He had learned to be gentle.

The Apostle Paul was another character that mellowed as time went on. Early in his ministry, Paul separated from a missionary named Barnabas because of a young man named John Mark. Mark had gone on a missionary trip with Paul and Mark's cousin Barnabas. While they were on the trip Mark left and returned to Jerusalem.[53] On their next trip, Paul became angry because Barnabas wanted to again take Mark. They went their separate ways.

Years down the road when Paul was on the last leg of his life before being put to death in Rome, he wrote to his apprentice, Timothy. In 2 Timothy 4:11, Paul requests Mark to join him because he was profitable for ministry. Paul's feelings against this young man were so strong that they split up one of the first missionary teams in existence. After Paul had matured in Christ, he mellowed and softened, requesting Mark because Mark had turned out to be a blessing.

What do I do when the honeymoon is over?

It feels good to be young and in love. Couples sit together, snuggling with their little rose-colored glasses on, making eyes at one another. Then, they get married and begin to learn what the other is really like.

---

[53] Acts 13:13.

And, as life continues, the realities of life set in. Many couples are saddled with a mortgage or rent payments. Soon, the happy couple may find out that they are about to be blessed with a bouncing bundle of joy. She may morph from businesswoman to mom. His life style may change from nights out with the boys to telling stories and tucking the kids into bed. They no longer have googly eyes for each other, and they learn how to love each other in a deeper, more meaningful way. (Side note: We would call this agape love.) They now must work to make time for each other. The relationship is not flowing like it once did, and now it is a daily effort to continue that relationship.

Sadly, many couples never work through their problems when they are young. Instead they choose to ignore the problems by focusing on life's busyness. They now have careers, kids, debt, and friends, and their lives move further apart. They are now two people sleeping in the same bed but living two different lives.

Nevertheless, few couples recognize this separation until they are older. At that point the kids are out of the house, and time is closing in on retirement. The more time they spend together, the more they realize their differences. They begin to drive one another away.

In this scenario, they are still the same two people, but life events have changed them. Over time they have learned everything there was to know about one another. They know exactly what buttons to push and when to push them. The honeymoon was over a long time ago, and now they are trying to learn how to live with one another on a different level.

Now compare this to a person's relationship with God. When most people get saved, it is exciting. The new Christian wants to share the good news with everyone, family and friends. The individual reads the Bible daily and prays without ceasing. Sadly, as time goes on many Christians lose their zeal. They go to church and believe in God, but their passion has begun to wane. Their Bible sits on the bookshelf, gathering dust and so do their prayer lives.

Just as the distance between a husband and wife can widen as they get older, our walk with God can drift, too. As the Spirit begins to mellow out our rough edges, it is important to keep in mind that we have to pay extra attention to our relationship with God. It may feel good to slip into a rut with God, but it is very difficult to get back out of one. Spiritually, we may no longer be in the honeymoon phase anymore, but we need to continue to tend the fire lest we wake up one morning and realize that we have let the coals burn out.

I once heard an aged minister say that he never felt far from God. These words were very discouraging to me, because I have gone through times in my life when I was discouraged and felt like God was a million miles away. Even as a preacher, I hit those walls from time to time. After praying about this, I believe God gave me the answer. It was not that the aged minister never felt like I did, rather he was secure enough in his relationship with God that he never really thought of God as being distant even when he was discouraged. That realization helped and encouraged me.

Whatever stage of a relationship that we are in, we must be careful. In the exciting time of the "honeymoon" we can become disillusioned, and as we begin our walk through the situations of real life, we can become disappointed. In the middle time of the relationship, when we should be growing into a deeper intimate love, we could begin to grow apart, instead. This time of mellowing and aging is invaluable and is a fruit that is borne in our lives, but we need to be cautious not to let down our guard. We should continue our commitments to the relationship that we have with God. No allowing ourselves to waver, but focusing on the truth of His love for us.

Chapter 17 – The Fruit of Goodness

We move on to the next fruit that the Spirit bears in the spirit of the Christian. In the King James Version it is translated as goodness. The Greek word used here comes from the word for "good" which is *agathos*. It is used only four times in the New Testament, and each time it is found in a book written by Paul.[54]

Goodness can mean many different things to many different people, because the English word takes on many characteristics. It can be used to describe a person's nature, and it can also describe a person's actions. One's understanding is dependent on that definition.

What does goodness mean?

Theologian and Bible Scholar John MacArthur reminds us of the story of Mary and Joseph.[55] Mary became pregnant, and Joseph was left with a very hard decision. He was concerned about marrying her because it seemed that she had been unfaithful, but he was a good man and did not want to disgrace her. So, he chose to essentially divorce her secretly. The

---

[54] George, Timothy, *Galatians,* Electronic ed. Logos Bible Software; the New American Commentary, vol. 30 (Nashville: Broadman and Holman Publishers, 2001, c1994), p 403.

[55] MacArthur, John, *Galatians* (Chicago: Moody Press, 1996, c1987), p 168.

accepted penalty in Jewish law for unfaithfulness was stoning. Joseph had every right to have Mary stoned but chose to show grace. MacArthur points out that Joseph was upright in character.

The Spirit's character is upright or righteous by nature. Just as the flesh is inherently evil, the Spirit is inherently good. It seeks goodness and righteousness. The Spirit seeks actions that line up with the will of God. Allowing the flesh to overrule the Spirit leads to evil actions, but if the Spirit overrules the flesh, then the resulting actions will be moral. There is not a set formula for what constitutes goodness in a Christian life. Instead, Christians should live according to the Word of God by allowing the Spirit to manifest His holiness.

The Jews had turned righteousness into a set of rules and regulations. God gave them the law as a model for life. They took this foundation and used it as a basis for the creation of a restrictive and prolific set of rules to live by. It is so easy for Christians to feel they can get a similar set of rules to help them feel more religious. Instead, Paul said that we have freedom and liberty.

As was discussed in chapter eight, we were created to do good works in our original state. With the fall of humanity, our original holiness was lost until the coming of the Holy Spirit. The Spirit of God does not give us a list to follow; rather, He gives us the ability and desire to live for God, not through our own abilities but through His own righteousness.

What is the difference between goodness and gentleness?

The two fruits, gentleness and goodness, seem to have a lot in common. Gentleness is demonstrated through kindness, and goodness is demonstrated through benevolence. However, the fruits are very different.

It is almost like comparing apples to oranges. While gentleness is a mellowing of personality, goodness is an action.[56]

Essentially, as the spirit dwells in our lives, it begets love. Love helps to temper our personalities by rounding off the rough edges and mellowing our attitudes. Love also promotes goodness in our lives which is demonstrated by acts of benevolence. Naturally, these related fruits work together for a common goal and promote the spirit-filled life.

What is important about benevolence?

Furthermore, goodness flows from the Christian because of the love and faith that he or she has. In other words, goodness leads us to act in generosity and benevolence, showing love for those around us.[57] Jesus dealt with this issue in Matthew 5:41 when he said, "When someone asks you to go with him one mile, go two."[58] Benevolence is generosity with no thought of reciprocation. Many people are generous because of what they hope to receive in return. Nevertheless, Christians are called to exhibit love and compassion with no expectation in return.

In Luke 6:34-35, Jesus contrasts the world's attitude with what He desired from his disciples. He spoke of giving to others. He said, "Don't give to others expecting a return, but give expecting nothing in return." True benevolence is practiced when a person acts altruistically with no motives or expectations

---

[56] Friberg, p 30.

[57] Bruce, F. F., *The Epistle to the Galatians: a Commentary on the Greek Text*, (Grand Rapids: W.B. Eerdmans, 1982), p 253.

[58] George.

If a person does good things merely for what he or she will receive, the acts are not motivated by love but by selfishness. Instead, God called us to love unselfishly, without limits. Therefore, generosity that is motivated by the desire for personal gain is not true goodness. Our goodness should flow from us because of the work of the Spirit inside of us.

Have you ever noticed during Jesus' discussion of the true vine in John 15 that he focuses on love? He says, "As the father loved me, I also have loved you, continue forth in my love." Then He discusses the commandment, "Love one another." Wrapping up the discourse He states, "You have not chosen me, but I have chosen you and ordained you that you may bring forth fruit."

Goodness and benevolence are byproducts of love. They naturally flow freely from the lives of those who are wholly committed to God and abide in the vine. While the branch bears the fruit, the vine is the life force.

What does our motive have to do with goodness?

In Luke 18:9-14, Jesus tells a story of two men who were praying in the temple. One was a Pharisee, the other a tax collector. These two men were complete opposites in the view of society. The religious people of the day diligently followed the many statutes of the Jewish law. They did everything correctly as far as the law was concerned. They wore the right clothes and had the right families. Many Jews esteemed Pharisees and other religious teachers and considered them perfect and righteous by human standards.

On the other hand, tax collectors were hated and ridiculed by their contemporaries. Many tax collectors were crooks. As they collected taxes for Rome, they would extort kickbacks and inflate the rates, sending to

The Fruit of Goodness

Rome the taxes that were required and keeping the excess for themselves. Even honest tax collectors were considered vile because they were Jews who were working for the Romans. No one wanted to associate with a tax collector.

While the Pharisee stood in the middle of the temple, he prayed, "Lord, thank you that I am not like others--extortioners, unjust, adulterers, or even this tax collector." The Pharisee then began to list the "righteous" things that he did, like fasting and giving his tithes and offerings. The Pharisee made sure that he was seen by others in the temple. He was loud and obnoxious and pointed out the sins of others to make himself appear better before God.

On the other hand, across the room, the tax collector knelt by himself. He did nothing to call attention to himself. He did not care about the others in the room. Feeling unworthy, he would not even raise his eyes to Heaven, but, rather, beat his chest while he cried out, "I am a sinner, have mercy."

We can see by this illustration that the world has a different definition of what it means to be righteous. In the eyes of the people, the Pharisee would have appeared righteous and holy. But in the eyes of Jesus, the Pharisee was arrogant. People would have considered the tax collector a sinner and "sellout"; however, Jesus recognized the humility in this man. Of the two men, Jesus stated that the tax collector left justified.

In this story we also find two very different motives. The Pharisee's motive was to receive acclamation from those around him. Seemingly, he cared more about what people thought than what God thought. The tax collector did not seem to care what the world thought; he only wanted to make a connection with God.

Our motive is pivotal to our spiritual goodness. A person who gives to be recognized is giving for the wrong reason. But a person who gives because of his love for God and the desire to see a difference in people's lives, has a pure motive. Goodness has little to do with what people see in our actions, because it comes from the Spirit working in the heart.

In 1 Samuel 16, Samuel was looking to anoint a new king. The first Hebrew king, Saul, had been the epitome of a king. He looked the part and acted the part. Nevertheless, he failed to honor and obey God. So, God sent Samuel to find someone to take his place on the throne. Samuel followed God's directions and went to Bethlehem to meet with Jesse and Jesse's sons. One by one, Jesse called his sons to be presented to Samuel. Samuel saw the traits of each son, recognizing each as a possible candidate. Nonetheless, God recognized only one. He was the youngest, a simple shepherd boy, and the most unlikely candidate to be the next king.

In verse 7, God tells Samuel, "The Lord does not see as man sees, for man looks on the outward appearance, but the Lord looks at the heart." God does not declare someone righteous because of the outward appearance and actions; rather, He looks at what is on the inside. In the same way, when dealing with us, He looks at the heart and the motives behind our actions.

What does motive have to do with standing upright before the Lord?

Upon examining the prayers of the Pharisee and the tax collector, we discover that honesty was probably the greatest difference. The Pharisee did not see himself as he truly was. He believed the lie that he was better than other people, and he enjoyed the praise of men. The tax collector realized that he was a sinner and was unworthy of grace but trusted that God would have mercy.

The men's prayers did not make them righteous. Instead, the motives behind their words determined their state of righteousness before God. Of the two, only the tax collector stood righteous and justified because he was honest with himself and sought approval from God instead of the world.

In Genesis 17:1, God tells Abram how to stand in righteousness and goodness before God. God instructed him, "Be thou perfect." At first glance it appears that God is telling Abram to live perfectly, which all of us would say is impossible to do. Nevertheless, in Hebrew and Greek, the words for "perfect" mean complete, upright, unimpaired, and sincere.[59] God asked Abram to be honest, sincere, and complete. Abram was not perfect, throughout his life. He lied when he told the Pharaoh and, later, King Abimelech that Sarah was his sister instead of his wife. He slept with his wife's handmaid, Hagar to give God a hand in providing him with a son. Also, he and Sarah doubted that God could do what He had promised and laughed when they were told that she would conceive a child in her old age. Nevertheless, he was sincere, and ultimately trusted God to bring His promises to pass.

In Hebrews 11, Abraham (Abram) is declared righteous not because of his actions, but because of his faith. In the same way, as the Spirit brings goodness into our lives, our actions change to make the world a better place. Through our motives and our faith in God, He declares us righteous.

---

[59] Strongs, H8549.

Chapter 18 – The Fruit of Faithfulness

The fruit of faith is a little peculiar. The word used here is *pistis* which comes from the Greek work *peitho*[60] which means to persuade or gain one's trust. While most commentators agree that the fruit of faith refers to faithfulness, there are those Bible scholars[61], especially from contemporary protestant and Charismatic churches, who interpret the fruit of faith as depth of belief. Just as there is a difference of opinion among scholars, there is also a difference in interpretation among local pastors and spiritual leaders. For this reason, to apply both understandings we will be examining both sides of the word to help better comprehend how it may be used to describe both scenarios.

What is true faithfulness?

Faithfulness is a very important word especially in the twenty-first century. We hear so much about unfaithfulness that it is easy to become disheartened with the realization that the world is full of unfaithful people. This lack of sincerity and trustworthiness has resulted in the decline of committed "until-death-do-us-part" relationships. God, on the other hand,

---

[60] Strong, G4102.

[61] Hamon, 131.

The Fruit of Faithfulness

is always faithful, and He takes care of His people. If we have the Spirit of a faithful God dwelling inside of us, then we can become faithful in an unfaithful world.

Basically, a faithful person is one that another can put his or her trust in. That person is worthy of our faith. Just as God can be trusted in the spiritual realm, we should be worthy of trust to those who depend on us as well. Since faith is used primarily on a spiritual or religious level, a better term may be trust. When we are faithful, people can put their trust in us. Furthermore, to better understand what it means for us to be faithful, we need to understand how God is faithful to us, since we are his representatives to the world.

First, God is faithful to keep his promises. In the Deuteronomy 7:9, it says that God is God, and He keeps the covenants that He makes to those who follow Him. God is unwilling to break his covenants. Whether it was the promise that God would give Abram a son, the promise that God would give the children of Israel a home, or the promise that He would let His people return home from exile, God was faithful to keep his promises. Hebrews 10:23 reminds us to hold fast to the promises of God because He who made those promises is faithful.

In the same way, our words should also be faithful. In Matthew 5:37, Jesus said to let your "Yes" be yes and "No" be no. In other words, instead of swearing with an oath, we should just say what we mean and mean what we say. When we agree to do something, we do it. The quickest way to lose someone's trust is by letting him or her down by not following through with what we have declared to be true. Since we are His representatives, when we let people down, our actions reflect poorly on the character of God.

Secondly, God is faithful to keep his children from the evil one. In 2 Thessalonians 3:3, it declares that God is able and works faithfully to keeps us. Even in rough times, He keeps us from being overpowered by the enemy. He is the friend that sticks closer than a brother[62].

We, too, can show this type of fellowship with others by continuing to walk in harmony, showing love, and uplifting one another in times of need. It is easy to walk away when the going gets tough, but with the help of the Spirit, we can remain faithful to one another even when it is difficult. When the world walks away, we can remain committed and trustworthy.

Additionally, God is faithful to forgive. In 1 John 1:9, it says that we can repent for our trespasses and believe because God is faithful to forgive what we have done. In Lamentations 3:23, it says that His mercy is new every morning and his faithfulness is great. God is faithful and just; He forgives our sins. Even when we were yet sinners, Jesus died for our sins.[63] He brought unconditional love and forgiveness for our iniquities.

In the same way, we can also offer forgiveness to those who have hurt us. Through the Spirit of God, we can be faithful to forgive others. When we are wronged, we can either hold on to the hurt and maintain the anger, or we can choose to ask God to help us forgive and work through that anger. It is not easy, and it does not mean that we put ourselves in the same place to be hurt again. Instead, it means that we do not hold the person spiritually accountable and let God help us move on.

Since the Spirit is alive and well in our hearts, it is important to allow the Spirit to make us more like God. Just as God is faithful to us, we

---

[62] Proverbs 18:24.

[63] Romans 5:8.

should be faithful to others. When we demonstrate faithfulness, the world can see who God is, and better understand what it means to be a Christian.

How can I grow to be faithful?

Being faithful is not always the easiest thing to do. When I was a child, I was taught that my reputation was very important, and the way people looked at me was affected by how I acted. Nevertheless, everyone breaks promises or is unable to live up to the standard that they have set. As a teacher, I see many students that easily throw around the word "promise" or "I swear". Usually, when most of these students get what they want, they no longer feel obligated to keep their commitment. Whether it involves a relationship, friendship, or even a classroom assignment, many children are not taught to follow through on their commitments.

Furthermore, we can also limit our abilities to be faithful by overextending ourselves. When we feel pressured or obligated to do something, it is easy to make a promise we are unable to keep. For this reason, we should always know our own limits. We do not have to commit to things we will not have time to accomplish.

As a minister, it easy for me to feel obligated to load my schedule with everything I am asked to do. I have a family; we have foster children; I work in a school and a church. I also lead worship on an Air Force Base, and write, amongst other things. When someone asks for help it is hard to say, "no". Nevertheless, we must be aware of our limits. When we overextend ourselves, we are not able to remain faithful to anyone. Then people may lose trust in us, and it damages our reputations.

Therefore, we find that faithfulness is a trait that must be taught and must be cultivated. We must learn how to be trustworthy even if it means we must let some people down in the process. As with any other fruit of the Spirit, faithfulness takes time to develop, and it takes effort that we sometimes do not want to make. Nonetheless, it is worth it in the end.

What about having faith?

How can we have salvation without faith? How can we have a healing without faith? No matter the work that Jesus did on the cross, if we do not believe it, it will have no value for us. But how often do we allow faith to be our foundation? We would rather worry and fret about the problems of life than to have faith in God to take care of us. It is difficult in the fast-paced world in which we live for us to give in and let God be God. We feel that we can add to the solution by trying to take care of it ourselves, but all we do is get in the way.

Imagine a surgeon performing heart surgery while the patient is awake and trying to assist the doctor. No one would want that. Why then do we try to assist God? He says, "Come to me all who are weary and heavy laden, and I will give you rest. Take my yoke upon you."

Is God almighty? Can he do everything? Then why do we try to assist him? We act like He needs our help because He is unable to do it on His own. If we do not have faith, then God is not able to fulfill his will in us. God is limited by the box we put Him in. He is only able to provide as much as we will let Him achieve in us.

When Jesus entered Nazareth, as recorded in Mark 6, He had the chance to minister to the people in His hometown. His family and childhood friends were there, so, logically, one would think they would want to see the miracles that Jesus was doing. On the Sabbath he entered the synagogue and began to teach. But instead of being elated, the people were troubled. They asked each other, "Where did this man get the word's that he is saying? Is not this the carpenter, the son of Mary, and his siblings still live in the town?"

As Jesus left, he said, "A Prophet it not without honor, except in his hometown."[64]

Jesus had all power in heaven and earth. He could have accomplished anything they needed. However, since they did not believe in Him, Jesus was unable to do the miracles that He performed in many other towns. Unless faith is active in a situation, God limits His work.

In Hebrews 11:1, we read, "Faith is the substance of things hoped for." Faith gives mass and substance to the ephemeral vapor of our hopes. While hope is short lived, and like a vapor, it is quickly gone, Faith provides security and trust providing us the strength to hold fast to the God's promises.

To better understand the work of faith, I decided to analyze this verse a little more in depth. I began to look at the Greek meanings, and something new came into my heart. It stoked the fire inside of me giving me a new outlook on faith.

The Greek word *hupostasis*[65], translated in the KJV as "substance," refers to a foundation that can be built upon and brings stability. It also

---

[64] Mark 6:5.

[65] Strong, G5287.

means assurance and confidence. The word *elpizo*[66] means hope and expectation. To me hope is ephemeral. Our hopes quickly change and have no surety. There is no confidence in hope. So, with this in mind, I have retranslated this passage, "Faith is the confident assurance of what we expect." Still not wowed? Let me explain what that means.

How can I have confidence in God?

Confidence is the assurance that we know beyond a shadow of a doubt that God is all-powerful. It is the ability to trust that He will work and take care of each situation as it comes into play in our lives. We can be confident and know that He is God, and as God, He will move on the behalf of His people.

My sons ask me for a snack, and they trust that I will not give them something that is poisonous. They trust me. We took my oldest son in for his three-year checkup, and he had to get a shot. He was the bravest little boy that I had ever seen. He wanted to cry, but he was doing everything to hold it in. We had been talking it up for days. We encouraged him by telling him that he had to have it so that he would not get sick and that it would only hurt for a minute. He sat there without fighting us. He was a real trooper. Fear was in his face, but he knew that Mommy and Daddy were with him, and we were doing what we felt was best. He trusted us, just like we need to trust God.

Jesus said, "If your son asks for bread would you give him a stone, or if he asks for a fish would you give him snake?" If we do good things for our children and we are sinners, think of how many more good things

---

[66] Ibid, G1679.

The Fruit of Faithfulness

God will do for us, and He is the almighty God. But we must be assured of that. No matter how good God is, if we are not confident and believe that He is faithful to keep His Word, every promise rings hollow in our spirits.

Faith is built on trust. As I said a few minutes ago, *hupostasis* refers to a foundation. The integrity of the building depends on its foundation. If the foundation fails, then the structure fails. Nonetheless if the foundation is strong, the building can remain firm. Our confidence in God comes from our assurance that He is stable and secure. If we feel that God is unstable or capricious, then we will have no confidence in Him. On the other hand, if we trust in Him, we will be assured that He knows what is best.

Trust is one of the hardest things to earn, and even harder to regain if it is lost. God never fails, but humans fail. We relate to what we know to be true. Since our feeble minds cannot wrap around the fact that God is omnipotent, it is hard for us to trust Him. People fail us all the time, and we transfer that failure to God and feel like He will fail us, too.

For instance, I have always liked helping in the food booth at Vacation Bible School. One night I asked the children, "Has anyone ever had someone break a promise to you?" We had well over sixty kids that night, and in each class every hand went up. We all know what it is like to be disappointed. No matter how much we try to avoid it, people let us down. Even though the Word promises over and over that He is faithful, we can easily believe the lie that God is not willing to help us or take care us in our time of need. Nevertheless, He will never ever fail us. No matter what, we can always trust Him. It may look like the wrong decision at first, but if we just trust God, He will take care of us.

I am reminded of the story in the Gospels where Jesus was sleeping in the bottom of the boat while a storm was raging around them, and his disciples were up on top rowing as hard as they could to keep the boat moving. Suddenly, a disciple ran down into the bowels of the boat and said, "Jesus don't you care? We are all about to die!"[67]

Jesus was not angered by their concern, instead He stepped out on the deck, stretched out his hands and said, "Peace, be still." Then He walked up to the disciple and said, "Why were you fearful? How is it that you had no faith?" He was not angry. He just could not understand why they did not trust Him.

They had walked with Him daily, seeing all the miracles that Jesus had performed. Nevertheless, they just could not comprehend just exactly who was riding out the waves with them. Even up until the moment of his crucifixion, the disciples were unable to truly grasp the work that Jesus was doing.

Can I really expect God to do something for me?

Expectation is the difficult word. Most people experience a negative reaction to the word "expectation". At one time or another we have all had our hopes up and then been disappointed. I even had one parishioner say, "Expectation is just premeditated disappointment." I understand that sentiment because expectation in something that we have no assurance of, it can indeed be premeditated disappointment. However, in Christ we have assurance. We are not just expecting something to happen; we are putting our trust in the promises that God has given to us. He is faithful to keep His promises.

---

[67] Mark 4:38.

We know the characteristics of God because we know the characteristics of love. The Bible tells us what we can expect. Faith is the confident assurance in what we can expect from God. We do not have to worry because we trust in Him.

There are many things that we can expect from God. We can expect to be loved. The Word tells us that God loves us so much that He gave His only begotten son. We also expect to live forever with Him. It says that whosoever believes in Him will not perish but have eternal life. We also can expect forgiveness. His blood was shed so that we could be forgiven and set free from the things that keep us captive.

We also can expect to be blessed. The church has lost its understanding of blessing. People have perverted the idea of blessing to mean wealth and health but being blessed simply means to be enlarged. He can choose to bless us physically and with health, but only if we allow Him to bless us spiritually. God blesses us so that we can bless others. When God blesses us financially, He expects us to bless others with our money. He never wanted His people to have barns filled to the brim. Instead, God wants our surplus in every area of life to always be flowing out of us and into others. We should be letting God's blessings flow out so that we can be ready for the harvest.

In addition, we can also expect to live life abundantly. If a glass is filled to the top, it is full, but when it begins to spill out over the top, that is abundance. The abundance is the overflow. As God pours into us, we pour out into others.

Moreover, abundance is not the same for everyone. For some people abundance is great wealth that they can use to bless the church and provide for the needs of others. For other people, it is enough extra food on the table to help the family next door who does not have enough. Just like God will not give us more than what we can bear, He will not bless us with more than we can handle.[68]

Sadly, some people choose to use the blessing that God gives them to take them away from God. He blesses them so that they can do His will, but they selfishly horde the blessing for themselves and move farther away from God.

I remember hearing a story about a woman who did not have a car and always got a ride to church. She was there without fail. The Pastor's son was buying a new car, and his old car was in very good condition, so he gave the car to this mighty saint of God. That Sunday she was not at church. She was absent the following Sunday, too. After a few weeks, the pastor was able to catch her at home. He asked her if everything was alright. She replied, "I have never had a car, and now, since I have a car, I went to visit my kids last weekend and my sister the weekend before." She had been given a blessing so that she could make it to church, and she allowed it to hinder her from attending the house of God.

We can expect God to be faithful to us, but we also must remain faithful to him. No matter what we are trusting Him for, if we are not being faithful to God, we limit what He is able to do in our lives. For this reason, we must continue to growth faithfully.

How do we build faith?

We build our faith through constantly being reminded of what God is doing in us. The first chapter of Psalms says that the righteous meditate

---

[68] 1 Corinthians 10:13

The Fruit of Faithfulness

on His commands. The word for meditate means to chew on it as a cow chews its cud. A cow chews and chews, then swallows. It then regurgitates the cud and begins chewing it again. Similarly, we take the word of God in and then continually bring it to mind and work through it. The Word of God should be regularly before us, molding us and making us new.

Abraham built his faith through confession. Previously, Abraham had been called "Abram". That was the old name, representative of the old man. As soon as God changed his name, he put aside his old identity and took on his new identity. The name his parents had given him meant "exalted father," and his new name meant "father of a multitude." With his new identity, every time his wife called him, she was essentially saying, "Father of a multitude, get in here and eat your Brussels sprouts," or "Father of a multitude, wake up! You forgot to milk the cows." As he took on the new identity, the more he heard his name, the more that identity embedded itself in his mind.

Consequently, the Word says in Romans 10:17, "Faith comes from hearing, and hearing from the Word of God." That means, we believe what we continually hear, and faith is developed when we continually hear the Word of God. The more we hear something, the more it gets into our minds, and then the more it gets into our hearts.

For instance, a child who lives in an abusive home, who continually hears how stupid he or she is will begin to believe that he or she is stupid. On the other hand, if a child is complimented and encouraged, the child will believe that he or she is able to accomplish anything. That child will prove it to be so. In the same way, spiritually, if we feed our minds the truth of God, the more we will believe that truth and the more we will grow in faith. So, for faith to grow, we should allow the Word to penetrate our minds, because what goes into our minds will move to our hearts.

How do faith and faithfulness work together?

Since the word *pistis* can mean both faith and faithfulness, there must be a connection between the two. Though the preferred interpretation in the listing of the fruits of the Spirit is faithfulness, there must be a link between being faithful and having faith. Author and Biblical authority N.T. Wright wrote, "Faith and obedience are not antithetical. They belong exactly together. Indeed, very often 'faith' itself could properly be translated as 'faithfulness', which makes the point just as well."[69] In other words, while many times people treat faith and putting one's faith into action as opposite poles, the two should not be separated. Faithfulness is nothing without faith. We cannot be faithful spiritually to God or anyone else without first believing in God. It is, therefore, our faith that begins the process of our faithfulness.

Again, the Apostle Paul's writing lends to the interpretation of the Spiritual fruit as faithfulness, but it is just as important that Christians grow in faith to truly develop in faithfulness. As we grow in faith, our faith is put into action and we can be true examples for Christ Jesus. In James 2:17 (NLT) it says, "…faith by itself is not enough. Unless it produces good deeds, it is dead and useless."[70] Our faith alone does not build a deeper

---

[69] Wright, N.T., *What Saint Paul Really Said,* (Grand Rapids: Eerdmans Publishing Company, 1997) p 190.

[70] Tyndale House Publishers, *Holy Bible: New Living Translation,* (Carol Stream, IL: Tyndale House Publishers, 2013).

relationship with God, but when we combine our belief with our faithfulness in action, we will grow closer to Christ.

Chapter 19 – The Fruit of Meekness

The next fruit of the Spirit is the fruit of meekness. Meekness is possibly one of the most misunderstood fruits of the Spirit. Most people equate meekness with timidity or weakness. It is often portrayed as softness, being mild-mannered, and poor. The church throughout history has taught congregants to be polite, easy to be manipulated, and unwilling to stand for what they believe. Sadly, many people have abused their power in churches and maintained control by implying that God's judgment is against anyone who was unwilling to be submissive. People were taught not to buck authority; they were kept poor and weak so that they would not grow to think for themselves. That is not what meekness means according to God's Word.

Who is called the meekest person?

Numbers 12:3 says that Moses was very meek, even above all others on the face of the earth. Since this phrase about Moses has little to do with the passage around it, some people believe that it may have been added later in history from the original writing. Also, the statement is parenthetical

The Fruit of Meekness

therefore many translations use parentheses to designate the phase as such.[71]

The word used in this phrase about Moses is not the typical Hebrew word used for humility or meekness. Instead, it is a word that means "total dependence on God."[72] We find this illustrated in Moses' statement to God when he was first commissioned to go to Pharaoh. In Exodus 3:11, he asked, "Who am I that I should go to pharaoh?" Moses knew that, in himself, he could not do the work that needed to be done. Moses could only act as God saw fit. He would not and could not act on his own. Rather he was fully dependent upon God.

Meekness and humility come from the acknowledgement that we cannot accomplish what needs to be accomplished by ourselves. No matter how hard we try, we cannot do anything good. Romans 3:10 says, "There is none righteous, no not one." Verse 12 then quotes Psalms 14:3 that says, "There is none that doeth good, no not one." In our own abilities, we are unable to be righteous, yet through the help of the Spirit, God makes us righteous.

Several years back, I heard a minister tell a story. He was preparing for a great revival and healing service. He put his name on the sign followed by the words, "Healing Crusade." As the sign was being raised, the minister peered up at the sign. He felt like God asked him, "Why is your name on the sign?"

In his mind the man replied, "It's my revival."

Then he felt God respond, "Good luck with that."

---

[71] Cole, R. Dennis, *Numbers,* electronic ed., Vol. 3B, (Nashville: Broadman and Holman Publishers, 2001, c2000), p 202.

[72] Ibid.

It is amazing to see what God can do through people, but we always must remember it is not us doing the work, but God who is working mightily through us. We are all instruments that God uses to do His will in the world. On his or her own, a singer cannot sing, and a preacher cannot preach. Any attempt on our own is feeble at best.

Legend tells us that the writer of Caedmon's Hymns, which told the stories of the Gospel in the English language, could not sing but had a desire to reach the lost. Caedmon earnestly sought God asking to be used. The story says that God blessed him with songs that played a part in spreading the Gospel to the common people of his time.

When people are willing to turn their hearts and lives over to God, He can do great things through them. When we are fully dependent upon His will and His work in our lives, we will be amazed at what He can achieve through us. Nonetheless, it takes complete surrender and reliance on him.

What does meekness have to do with submission?

The Greek word that is translated "meek" in the New Testament is the word *praos* or, as in Galatians 5:22, the derivative *praotes*. It means mild, meek, and gentle. The word was used in the past to describe a wild stallion that is taken in and tamed, so it can be trained be ridden.[73]

This is a much different picture than we typically get. Basically, *praotes* refers to an animal that retains its strength and its ability but has learned to be subservient to another. A horse is easily able to overpower its rider. Its massive stature could easily kill an adult, much less a child, but

---

[73] Walters, Kerry, *Merciful Meekness: Becoming a Spiritual Integrated Person*, (Mahwah, NJ: Paulist Press, 2004), p 37.

when it is trained properly, it follows the commands of its bit and bridle. A simple pull on the reins and the horse slows to a stop. A slight pull in one direction or the other leads the horse to turn.

Similarly, God wants to be able to lead and direct us. We have the same abilities, boldness, and strengths, but we are no longer acting on our own accord. As meekness develops in our lives, God can use the abilities that we have to bring about His will instead of our own selfish desires.

Look at the life of Moses. He was not weak by any means. He is the only man to break all the Ten Commandments at one time. Another time he argued with God until God changed his mind. Moses knew his strength but was willing to put his strength aside and be subservient because he trusted in God.

How do I bear meekness?

Meekness typically starts with humility. A humble person learns not to rely on him or herself and, instead, to rely on God. We need to overcome pride. Proverbs 16:18 says, "Pride goes before destruction and a haughty spirit before a fall." James says in 4:6, "God resists the proud and gives grace to the humble." When we allow pride to poison our minds, we begin believing that we can act in our own abilities instead of relying on the power of God.

When we sow humility, we choose to allow the needs of others to take priority over our own. By doing so, we no longer look to our own abilities. This act of humility will help us change our way of thinking and begin precipitating meekness in our everyday lives. Furthermore, we will learn ways to trust God's will instead of our own.

Chapter 20 – The Fruit of Self-Control

Self-control sounds like it would be one of the easiest fruits to obtain. Everyone should be able to control him or herself. Nevertheless, we have thousands of people in prisons, millions of people addicted to various substances, and almost everyone has some type of vice that exerts some degree of control from the outside. Self-control seems that it would be simple to maintain, but it is possibly one of the most difficult.

Controlling one's self requires more discipline and self-awareness than the other fruits of the Spirit. It requires that a person recognize his or her limits as well as being true to one's morals and values. When a person learns to recognize his or her limits, the individual can make appropriate choices to live within those limitations. However, this is just the tip of the iceberg.

To truly understand self-control, we will need to define the Greek word used for self-control. The word that is used in the Greek New Testament refers to one who masters his desires and passions, especially his or her sensual appetite.[74] In other words, self-control requires keeping one's desires and passions in balance. The King James Version translates it as "temperance", and it means to maintain moderation and sometimes to

---

[74] Strongs, G1466.

practice abstinence. Essentially, a person exhibiting self-control is one who practices moderation, who abstains from that which is impure, and is fully in control of him or herself.

What do we give our lives over to?

We give control of our minds and bodies to many things. Some people allow alcohol and other drugs to control them. Others turn to sex or pornography for self-gratification. Sadly, we do not set out to allow ourselves to be controlled by these things. For most people, it begins as a search for comfort or safe place. For instance, just as people turn to drugs and alcohol when life is rough, others over-indulgence when eating or waste exorbitant amounts of money to overcome feelings of inadequacy or depression.

In all these activities, the satisfaction is temporary and fleeting. People enjoy the initial high, but over time the things that caused pleasure are no longer able to satisfy. He or she is left looking for other avenues to gratify the desires. The need to fill the lonely places in our hearts can be found in every person, from the most well-respected Christian minister to the lowest "degenerate" strung out on a street corner. We all deal with problems, and how we deal with those problems typically relates back to the things we have experienced in our lives.

As a foster family, we see many children who struggle with anger and frustration. They become belligerent at times, because they do not understand what is happening. They cannot grasp why they have been pulled from the home they know and placed in another home. On several occasions we have had children placed with us who had actually taken on the role of parenting. The child cooked the food, watched the baby, and took care of any menial tasks around the home that needed to be done. When a child has been through such a situation, the child struggles with proper ways to respond and act when feelings overwhelm him or her. It is easy to fall into bad habits and let things control us when we do not have the needed tools to deal with life.

Moreover, this kind of situation can happen to anyone. There are people who were raised in good, strong, healthy homes and have families who love and support them, but who still end up suffering from addiction and lack of self-control. The issue of self-control is not an issue for only the poor and the rejected, but for every being human.

For instance, in the weeks leading up to the January execution of serial rapist and murderer, Ted Bundy, Doctor James Dobson had several interviews with Bundy in an effort to better understand the circumstances that led up to that day. These interviews have been considered by some to be controversial, as possibly an attempt to receive a stay of execution by Bundy and/or an attack on the porn industry by Dobson. In either case, the information that this family psychologist gathered has helped to open the eyes of many on the damaging effects of the use of pornography. Furthermore, for many people, the use of pornography is an initial step to engaging in inappropriate sexual relationships.[75]

For Bundy, and many other serial killers, the initial impetus or catalyst was a brief glance, but its ultimate consequence was devastation, death and destruction. Most people feel they would never find themselves

---

[75] Bundy, Ted, interview by James Dobson, *Fatal Addiction: Ted Bundy's final interview* (January 23, 1989).

in such a place, but every sin that we struggle with begins small and grows over time. When we allow ourselves to falter, even once, self-control becomes more difficult.

How do we act in moderation?

Not all actions are inherently wrong. Rather, all actions, even the most benign, should be practiced in moderation. For instance, eating and sleeping are primary functions of the human body, but when someone consistently eats too much or tries to sleep all day every day, he or she may have a problem with self-control. Moderation means to be aware of one's limits instead of overindulging. No matter what the act, we must be mindful and maintain a healthy balance.

Recently there has been a new breed of alcohol commercials on television. I remember one that shows the host of the party taking the keys from everyone when he or she entered the party. In another commercial the host has a large remote control, and if anyone tries to leave the party, he runs over the person's vehicle with a monster truck.

To release themselves from the liability for the consequences of the actions of drunken patrons, several alcohol companies have adopted slogans like "drink responsibly" or "always in moderation." It is stated in the commercials and listed on the bottles and cases. The effort is being made to keep people from allowing alcohol to control them and doing something that he or she would not normally do.

When people ask me, "Why can't I get drunk?", I tell them, "When you get drunk, you are not in control of yourself and are turning control over to something else." It is the same with drugs. When a person chooses to partake in actions that will impair his or her judgment, that person willingly chooses to forfeit control.

While hospitals and lawyers will not allow a person, who is on certain pain medications to make decisions about his or her well-being, people choose to make decisions all the time while their judgment is affected by alcohol or drugs. When the person returns to his or her right mind, the person may, regretfully, discover what choices were made in an inhibited state. The consequences of many such choices are life-altering and cannot be undone.

Our lives must be tempered with moderation regarding relationships, work, eating habits, family, and so on. When we allow ourselves to focus more heavily on one area of life than another, we choose to be governed by some authority other than God. God wants to be the reigning champion of our lives; He is not willing to turn that influence and authority over to all the other things we may choose to put in the place that rightfully belongs to Him.

When should I practice abstinence?

Abstinence is a word that every teenager in church has probably heard millions of times and is now thought of as an overused buzzword. If I announce to a group of teenagers that I am going to be talking about abstinence, they will immediately zone out. The word itself has been used so often that many people try to avoid it all together, and the methods to promote sexual abstinence among students have often encouraged them make hollow promises they never intend to keep.

The Fruit of Self-Control

Nevertheless, abstinence can pertain to more than just sex. It simply means to not participate in certain activities. There are many things in the world that people should not touch: recreational drugs, pornography, etc.

We often hear about the horrible repercussions of drug use. The media, medical societies, and political leaders use drug abuse as a stance for change, but sadly, drug use continues to be an ever-increasing problem in our nation and in our world. We see how it ruins lives and families. It has even been described by some as an epidemic. Many people would consider it to be common sense to avoid using drugs, but for the millions already involved with drugs, it is an everyday battle.

Furthermore, with the onset of the internet, things like explicit relationships, pornographic use, and other actions that most Christians would deem as demeaning are common place. It is estimated that 21% of Christian men and 2% of Christian women believe they may be addicted to pornography use.[76] That does not include those who view it only occasionally. While the use of pornography among non-believers is considered much higher, there was no distinction regarding what was considered at addiction and what was considered occasional use.

We know that God wants us to refrain from murder, theft, extortion, and abuse, but we often dismiss other sins like gossip, wrath, disrespect for authority, hatred, and envy. When God looks at sin, he does not have a list of good sins and bad sins. While we as Christian's have

---

[76] Proven Men Ministries, *2014 Pornography Survey and Statistics,* December 29, 2015, http://www.provenmen.org/2014pornsurvey (accessed Sepember 15, 2018).

maintained a list of the really-bad-sins and not-so-bad sins, God continues to tell us that sin is sin, and He wants us to refrain from all of them.

Is there s difference between self-control and a sound mind?

Self-control also means to have a sound mind. Legally and medically, a sound mind basically means to have the capacity to think, reason, and understand for oneself. When we give our control over to something else, such as drugs, alcohol, or desire, we are choosing not to act out of a sound mind. When we choose to act out of fear, we also choose to abandon our sound mind.

Many of the problems that people suffer from are related to fear and anxiety. Fear can instigate aggression and anger, and can many times lead individuals to begin abusing drugs or alcohol as a form of self-medication. Furthermore, people who are hurting often suffer from guilt and shame which leads them to hurt others. It is a continual cycle that causes individuals to act erratically.

Fear causes us to say and do things that are out of character for us. Due to fear of rejection or consequence, people may choose to react in anger and frustration. Some people abandon all rationale when fear is involved. They attack others and even commit murder to avoid judgment. Fear is the greatest weapon that the enemy has.

In 2 Timothy 1:7, it says, "For God hath not given us a spirit of fear, but of power and of love and of a sound mind." That means God has given us the ability to think clearly. He does not want us left fighting fear and anguish by ourselves. Instead, God gave us the Spirit so that we can live with a sound mind and a clear way of thinking. Instead of yielding our thoughts and emotions to fear or sin, through the power of God we can maintain control of our hearts and minds. We can remain stability, trusting that our decisions are made rationally.

How do I grow in self-control?

Stop ignoring the signs. When the Spirit says, "Stop," then STOP. That is His job. He constantly helps us, guides us, and intercedes for us. He is looking out for us in everything we do.

Furthermore, if we know that we cannot partake in something with moderation, then we should avoid it altogether. When I counsel men who say, "I can't help lusting after the women I see in movies," I recommend they stop watching movies that contain sexually explicit scenes. If a person cannot eat supper in a restaurant that serves alcohol because he or she will fall to temptation, it is better to avoid that situation altogether.

Christ is strong where we are weak, but He gives us common sense, too. If we are weak in an area, then it is important to avoid that area. Recovering alcoholics need not go into a bar. If a person's friends cause him or her to sin, that person needs to get new friends. God has given us a plethora of ways to get help: counseling, anger management, or therapy. There is nothing wrong with getting assistance. I believe it was Bill Hybels who said that every person should regularly visit with a counselor for good mental health. It is not a sign of weakness to admit we have a problem; it is a sign of strength because we are willing to do what it takes to change.

PART 5
APPLYING THESE PRINCIPLES TO LIFE

> Being a Christian is more than just an instantaneous conversion – it is a daily process whereby you grow to be more and more like Christ.
>
> .
>
> --Billy Graham[77]

---

[77] Miller, Carmen. *Remembering Billy Graham: 20 Memorable Quotes.* February 21, 2018. http://www.wholemagazine.org/posts/remembering-billy-graham-20-memorable-quotes (accessed September 22, 2018).

Chapter 21 – All Wrapped up in Love

We began the discussion of the fruits of the Spirit by talking about love because it is listed first in Galatians 5:22. In this chapter we will be looking at the relationship that love has with the other fruits. We will also compare the purpose of love to the truth of the Gospel and see how love is intertwined in God's actions from the beginning of time.

What can be greater than love?

As we have mentioned previously, in 1 Corinthians chapter 12, Paul talks extensively about the gifts of the Spirit. He speaks of things like prophecy and wisdom. At the very end of the passage in verse 31, Paul said that he would demonstrate something that is greater than all the other gifts that God had given. He then begins what we call the "Love Chapter", 1 Corinthian 13. Though we will look at 1 Corinthians 13 in more depth in a moment, I want to bring out something seemingly contradictory about Paul's statement.

Many people would ask, "How is love greater than prophecy or healings?" I think the answer can be found in Jesus' words. Jesus says in John 13:34, "A new command I give to you that you love one another. As I have loved you, love each other." In 2 John 5, again John restates Jesus' decree, "Love one another." For a Christian, love is the greatest of all things. It is the basis of all Christianity.

How did God love us? God's love is transcendent. It is not bound by time or space, instead it exists in eternity. God's love extends through all of history and affects everyone. In John 3:16, it says, "God so loved the world." The Greek word translated for world is *kosmos* which means all of creation. The word is not limited to just a few people or a portion of the world, but the whole, sinful multitude. God did not love only those whom He knew would be saved; God loved everyone while we "...were yet sinners".[78]

God loves the world. He gave value to the world. Everyone in the world was worth the life of His Son, Jesus Christ. Jesus hung up his royal clothes and robed Himself in flesh, so he could come to earth to pay the sin debt for humanity.[79] His love was far superior to any love this world could ever offer. Moreover, in 1 John 4:19, we find that we should "...love him because he first loved us." Christ came to set the captive free, bring sight to the blind and preach the Word of good news unto the world (Luke 4:18).

Treasured versus Loved

In 1 Peter 2:9, God's people are referred to as a peculiar people. Now I have known some very strange, peculiar people, but the Biblical understanding of "peculiar" is "prized possession" or "treasured" This verse in Peter is reminiscent of Deuteronomy 14:2, where we find, "You

---

[78] Romans 5:8.

[79] John 1:14.

are a holy people to the Lord, out of all of the people on the face of the earth He chose you as a treasured people." Some translations of this verse use the term peculiar, as well, like the verse in 1 Peter. Moreover, the word "holy" means to be set apart for God's work. As peculiar people, we were chosen by God as his prized possession or treasure, set aside for his purpose.

We should always remember that God, who is not a respecter of persons, loves everyone. He loves you, your neighbor, your associate, your friends, your acquaintances, your enemies, and everyone else in the world. God loves the unrepentant man sitting on death row. However, there is a very strong difference between being loved and being treasured. It is a fine line, and the Word says that God treasures those who are His.

We find in Genesis that God set apart Abraham and his family. By the time of Moses, God had set aside the Hebrews as His chosen people. Later they were called the Israelites, and following the Babylonian Exile only the Southern part of the kingdom remained. From then on, they were referred to as Jews because they were made up primarily of the tribe of Judah. Still, God blessed them. Throughout the Bible God made covenants with them unlike those with any other nation of the world.

The Jewish nation was almost obliterated following the fall of Jerusalem and Herod's temple after a Jewish revolt in AD 70. Nevertheless, God remembered the Jews for almost nineteen hundred years, until he brought them back together as a nation. Following the Holocaust, the United Nations returned the Jewish people to their home in Israel. As previously mentioned, no other nation has lost everything, including their land, language, and heritage, and been able to return home and rebuild after almost two millennia. If God can do that work for the Jewish people, who had basically given up on the opportunity to return home, think of what He can do for us.

Why has Jesus not returned?

This question has been an issue with some Christians and non-Christians, alike. They wonder why it is that God waits and lets the world continue in its evil way. It is hard for us to understand how a just, righteous God could look at an unjust, unrighteous world and allow it to continue. Non-Christians have even used this as an attempt to disprove the existence of God.

By many, a just God who allows the ungodly to continue hurting others is considered a moral dilemma. Sadly, I have heard some use this as an excuse for turning away from the Gospel because people cannot comprehend God's reasoning. Others have blamed God for their pain and suffering.

However, we get a clue into God's heart in 2 Peter 3:9, where we find, "The Lord is not slack concerning his promise, as some men count slackness; but is longsuffering to us-ward, not willing that any should perish, but that all should come to repentance." God is not waiting as we think He is waiting. Instead, He is patient because He wants all to come to repentance.

Love is the most powerful force in the entire world. It was the force that led God to come to earth to die. It is the force that restrains His hand from judgment. It is the force that quickens our hearts to salvation. God is love.

How is God love?

In the earlier chapter about the fruit of love, we defined *agape* as unconditional, committed, pure love. This type of love is the closest thing we could experience to being like God. The more we learn about God's character, the more we will realize that God and true love share many of the same characteristics. Furthermore, in 1 John 4:8 the statement, "God is love" is grammatically reflective in the Greek language. That basically means that the two words could be switched in the statement. It could be inferred that they are synonymous.

The reason we cannot truly understand God is because we cannot truly understand love. We are too easily swayed by our emotions. We allow ourselves to get tied up in the way we feel, instead of what is real. I once heard someone say that fear is the opposite of love. I did not agree at first, but now I do. Fear is an emotional response. True love is independent of our emotions.

If God is love and the Holy Spirit is one with God, then that means that the Holy Spirit, also, is synonymous with love. Essentially, no one can ever experience true *agape* love without the Spirit of God. Furthermore, the Bible reminds us that it was the Holy Spirit that brought us to Christ, meaning love brought us to Christ. It is all about love. When we show love, we are showing the essence of God to a lost and broken world.

Is love essentially the only fruit of the spirit?

Everything we know about God is demonstrated in His love for us. For this reason, I cannot help but wonder if the fruits of the Spirit can all be encapsulated in love. This can be seen when we read 1 Corinthians 13.[80] The definition of love that we discover in Paul's writings to the church of Corinth lines up with his writing in Galatians 5:22. In the English translation almost every description of love found in the "love chapter" is essentially mentioned in the fruits of the Spirit. Both speak of joy, faith, meekness, kindness, and gentleness.

Even in the Greek translation several of the words are related. The Greek verb form of the word for faith is used in believing. The Greek words for gentleness and kindness come from a common derivative, as does the words for long suffering that are used in both. The characteristics of love are basically equivalent to the fruits of the Spirit.

Furthermore, the love chapter says directly that a person can have any gift of the Spirit, but if he or she does not have love, everything else is worth nothing. If true love is the essence of God working in our lives, all the other fruits of the Spirit can be related to love. It may even be all right to say that the other fruits are a byproduct of the fruit of love manifesting itself in our lives. As love is manifested in our lives, it will begin to touch the world around us.

---

[80] Spence-Jones, p. 262.

Chapter 22 – Corporate Fruit Bearing

Look in the book of Numbers, chapter 13, verse 23. We read about a giant cluster of grapes. It says that the spies who went into the Promised Land to check out the land came to an area that they called *Eshcol*, which means cluster. There they cut down a branch from a grape vine with a single cluster of grapes so large that it took two men to carry it.

God made a promise to Moses and the children of Israel that He would let them inherit the land that was owned by their fathers Abraham, Isaac, and Jacob. Some people call it the Promised Land; others call it Canaan's land, but it was the land of Israel.

Here in the book of Numbers, the children of Israel were standing right outside of the land of promise. They sent in twelve spies to check out the land. Ten of the spies came back with a negative report, and two came back with a positive report. Everyone agreed that the land was richly blessed and that it was filled with everything that the children of Israel would ever need. But the inhabitants of the Promised Land were mighty, and the cities were walled. The ten spies with a negative report said, "We are like grasshoppers in their eyes."

The children of Israel became terrified by this report. Joshua and Caleb were the only two that stood up and proclaimed the promise of God, but to no avail. The decision not to enter the land of Canaan cost the children of Israel forty years of wondering in the desert. By the time they were finally allowed to go into the Promised Land, the only two people left alive from that first generation were Joshua and Caleb.

Why did Israel have to wait to receive the promise?

The children of Israel had everything that they needed to enter the land of promise. They had the power and the numbers, but more importantly, they followed the Almighty who gave them the power to overcome. They did not inherit the land for forty years. They did not get the Promised Land at the time that God offered it to them. They suffered from a mob mentality, which means the individuals followed the leading of the crowd even when it went against their own convictions.

I remember the first time I saw the movie *Men in Black*. There is a scene where Tommy Lee Jones and Will Smith were working a case, and Smith asked why they could not tell the world about the existence of Aliens because, he said, "People are smart." Jones replied, "A person is smart, but people are stupid." It is sad but true. There are some people who are geniuses. An individual person can be very smart, but people as a group react very stupidly. There is something about fear that is multiplied when you get a group of people together. In youth we call this "getting on the band wagon" or "going along with the crowd."

As Christians, we tend to think that the children of Israel were foolish for not going into the Promised Land. We can even get pious and judgmental about it, but, sadly, there are many churches that miss out on the promises of God because of mob mentality. I heard recently about a church that was split down the middle because half of the church wanted a different color carpet than the other half. Petty, I know, but that sort of thing happens all the time. More churches split because of the petty things than the important things, and many of these churches ultimately have to close their doors.

The children of Israel had the promise of God in their grasp but missed it because they listened to the crowd instead of listening to the assurances of God. When God makes a promise, He will do the work to see it through. We do not have to worry, because He is trustworthy. God will take care of everything.

Sadly, we choose to act like Abraham. We would like to think that Abraham immediately believed God when God first promised him that he would bare a son. However, Genesis 17:17 says that Abraham laughed. I can imagine that he thought to himself, "Am I hearing this right? He thinks I will father a son when I am a hundred years old?" His initial reaction was much like ours would be. But, ultimately, he did believe, and he received the son of the promise God made him.

What voice are we listening to?

The children of Israel had everything they needed, but they lost the right to see the manifestation of God's promise. They listened to the voice of the flesh. We have talked extensively about the flesh and the Spirit. As we have stated many times, the flesh is self-satisfying and self-preserving, while the Spirit seeks after the things of God. Instead of listening to the voice that said, "You can do this; I have your back", they listened to the voice that said, "You are not strong enough; it is not worth the effort." A whole generation of people died with the epitaph that said, "It is not worth the effort."

It takes effort to produce. A farmer must work the land. He plants the seed and works to maintain the growth of the plants. Similarly, to be spiritually mature, we have to make the effort to build a relationship with God.

What voice are we listening to? The flesh says, "Oh, it won't hurt anybody, take a look, try it just once, no one will ever know." The Spirit is saying, "Retreat." We love the verse found in James 4:7, "Resist the devil, and he will flee from you." We tend however to overlook the verses that say, "Flee from fornication, flee from evil things, flee lusts of spiritual immaturity, flee from putting things before God." In all these cases, flee means to retreat or to run from. We are not supposed to flirt with evil. We are not supposed to be walking the line of temptation. We are supposed to get as far away from it as we can. When we walk on the edge, we have a greater chance of falling in than we do when we put a safe distance between ourselves and the temptation or vice that is trying to tempt us.

It is very easy to listen to the flesh. It is much harder to trust in God. When we listen to the flesh, we think we are watching out for ourselves, but God said He would watch out for us. Jesus said in Luke 17:33, "Whoever tries to preserve his life will destroy it, but whoever puts aside his life will be made alive." God is not asking us to sacrifice everything to Him. He just wants us to trust Him. When we do, we will find that we are truly living.

Corporate Nature

Every creature wants to be part of something greater. Wolves run in packs, lions in prides, birds in flocks, and people in families. Author and poet John Donne wrote in Meditation Seventeen, "No man is an island, entire of itself; everyone is a piece of the continent, a part of the main." Simply put, to have a successful life, people need others. Speaker Roy C. Cook adds to this thought saying, "Every man is an island, but there is no limit to the bridges or harbors one can build."[81] In other words, while people are separate and distinct, they still desire relationships and connections.

In the movie *Castaway*, Tom Hanks played an executive who was lost on a deserted island. He began going a little crazy due to the lack of social interaction. He found a volleyball on which he drew facial features and called it Wilson. Close to the end of the movie he was on a raft trying to make it home when he lost Wilson and was completely devastated. It may seem farfetched, but the truth is... we all need someone. We need friends and family. We need social interaction. People who choose to be hermits and recluses still have to rely on some type of social interaction, or they will likely lose their minds. Many do.

We also have the need to be a part of a corporate body. It is very sad when a Christian says, "I do not need to go to church; I listen to

---

[81] Tan, Paul Lee, *Encyclopedia of 7700 Illustrations : A Treasury of Illustrations, Anecdotes, Facts and Quotations for Pastors, Teachers and Christian Workers*, (Garland, TX: Bible Communications, 1996, c.1979), 3902.

preachers on TV, and I pray." We do not go to church for God's sake, but for our own. Church should involve fellowship together. The Greek word that translates as "church" is *ekklesia*, which means an assembly.[82] God did not form a Church whose members meet once a week for an hour in order to be able to check off some religious duty. Jesus instituted an assembly of believers who come together in His name to learn and grow, with the ultimate purpose of advancing God's Kingdom.

We need that "assembling of ourselves together". We cannot live the Christian life to its fullest without that fellowship. God created all the animals for company for Adam. But these beasts were inadequate companions for him, so God created a woman, taken from Adam's rib so the connection would be immediate and complete. There is an internal need in all of us to have someone else that will help us and support us in all areas of our lives. As the Bill Withers' song says, "We all need somebody to lean on."

Why did God choose a church?

While fellowship is vital, too many times people treat the church as simply another place to fellowship. The Lion's Club, Rotary Club, VFW, Woman's Auxiliary, as well as others, offer fellowship. What separates these organizations from the church? Why is the church so important?

The church is a fellowship organization of believers who come together to promote God's work in the world. In Matthew 18:20 Jesus said, "Where two or three are gathered together in my name, there I will be in the midst of them." The church is the only organization that Jesus died for.

---

[82] Strongs, G1577.

Since the church gathers to worship and to serve God, He meets them there. The church is not simply a social club. It is the place where people come to have an encounter with God. Though all churches perform their worship services differently, their goal is to encounter Him as God. That is why it is important to be involved in a church body. Hebrews 10:25 says, "Not forsaking the assembling of yourselves together, not like some are doing." There is a need for that corporate encounter with God.

Furthermore, we also need to be able to help one another. Ecclesiastes 4:9-10 says that two are better than one and if one person needs help the other can assist. However, if a person trips and falls when he or she is alone, there will be no one to help the individual up.

The writer goes on to explain why this assembling together is so important. The purpose of the church is to edify one another. Ephesians 4:12 says that the work of ministers (namely prophets, apostles, evangelists, pastors, and teachers) is to perfect the saints for the work of the ministry to edify the body of Christ. God gave gifts of ministers, so they could train and teach the members of the body how to be ministers.

Some people are not willing to put themselves under a pastor. The pastor is the shepherd of the church. He or she is the person to whom God gives the vision for the church. I am a pastor but I still look to pastoral friends and colleagues for help and mentorship.

How to produce on a larger scale?

The assembly works together to corporately produce fruit. Think about a winery with a large vineyard. It takes more than one cluster of grapes to make a bottle of wine. For a winery to be successful, it must have many plants that are all producing. God created the church to corporately produce. For example, we will not see revival with just one or two people praying for it. Revival comes only when the body corporately is seeking revival.

As each member of the body produces fruit, the church corporately produces fruit. The church is grounded in Christ. He is the vine and we are the branches. As branches we work together to grow the kingdom.

How do we work together to bear fruit?

When I was working to complete a Bachelor of Science degree in Religion, I chose to finish my final hours online. I had previous attended different universities trying to discover where I belonged. The one thing I missed with my online education was the interactions with the other students and the faculty. For this reason, when I began my Master of Divinity degree, I decided to commute to Seminary. To be successful, I needed the interaction with other students and professors.

Similarly, we develop through our interactions with other people. The connections we make at church and in our spiritual community help strengthen us. Proverbs 27:17 reminds us that as iron sharpens iron, so does one person sharpen another. We learn and grow from each other.

Each person has something to offer. I always tell my volunteers and have tried to make it a rule to live by; if you are weak in particular area, you need to surround yourself with those who are strong in that area. For instance, I am not good at coming up with ideas for outreach or evangelism, but I have a minister friend that has years of experience in evangelism. I can go to him to learn ideas and new techniques. A former mentor of mine taught me a long time ago that we are not strong in every area of ministry, so we should allow those who are strong to work where we are lacking or weak.

Most flowers have a stamen, or male reproductive part, and a pistil, or female reproductive part; but most cannot reproduce by themselves. Instead, the pollen from the stamen of one flower must be transferred to the pistil of another flower by insects such as bees or other animals. That is how plants and trees are pollinated.

In the same way, Christians should not attempt to grow alone. We work together with others, speaking encouraging words, and helping in times of need. We lean on one another to find strength. Christians who go to church and receive the support of others are stronger than those who never attend and feel that they can do well enough on their own. The strength that can be derived from interaction with other Christians can bring richness to us in our Christian walk.

How can we benefit from working together?

You have heard it said, "Two heads are better than one," and that is very true. I heard a preacher recently say that his ministry team gets together weekly and discusses the upcoming sermons. Different people with different areas of expertise offer different insights on ways to improve the sermon. Some think of videos, others bring illustrations, and others bring drama or choreography. The members join and use the strengths of each individual to improve the service and attempt to provide diversified lessons that will maximize evangelism.

If only one person is working, his or her creativity will be limited to his or her ability, but if several people work together, the creative talents of each one of them are combined. We bring out creativity and strength in with others when we work for the common goal.

Chapter 23 – No Fruit?

Throughout this book our main premise was found in the fifteenth chapter of John. In that chapter, Jesus talked with his disciples about bearing fruit. He says, "He that abideth in me and I in him, the same bringeth forth much fruit." Simply put, if we are truly abiding in Christ, he will empower us to bear fruit. There is no way to get around it. He goes on to say, "Without me you can do nothing."

This verse causes a problem. If we are abiding in Christ, we automatically will bear much fruit. Consequently, if we are not bearing fruit, it is because we are not truly abiding in Him. Jesus said in John 15:6, "If a man abides not in me, he is cast forth as a branch, and is withered; and men gather them and cast them into the fire and they are burned." In chapters seven and eight we talked extensively about pruning and purging branches from a plant. We said that pruning is a process of cutting away dead or diseased branches and purging is the burning and destruction of those branches.

How do people no longer hear God?

God is willing to work with us if we are sensitive to Him and His leading. However, the more we seek out the flesh, the harder our hearts become. The harder our hearts get, the farther away we are from God. If we are not careful, there will come a day that we are so removed from Him that He can no longer break through our hardened hearts.

Developmental Psychologists have studied a baby's reactions to various stimuli. In this research they have studied habituation. A baby that is subjected to a stimulus may be startled, but if she is subjected to that stimulus multiple times, she habituates or becomes desensitized to the stimuli. When I was in my second year of college, I lived forty-five miles away from the university that I was attending. I would drive in at 6:00 in the morning to go to work, then go to class, and then back to work. After a while I got so accustomed to the drive that I would arrive at work and not remember how I got there. It is called road hypnosis, or desensitization to the road being travelled.

The same kind of thing can happen to us spiritually. Have you ever noticed how we may find that the first time we commit a particular sin, we may find it very difficult to do, but the more we do it, the easier it becomes? That is because we are desensitizing ourselves to the voice of God. The deeper we get into sin, the farther we get away from God. King Saul is the poster child of "God desensitization". In chapter 6 and chapter 17 we discussed King Saul. He began as a mighty man of God that was head and shoulders above all others.

Over time, as the prestige and power of royalty consumed him, he began growing farther away from God. Finally, he found himself tormented by bouts of depression and anger. Not long before his life came to a tragic end, he was in a witch's home, begging her to conjure up the spirit of Samuel, who had died, so that he could find direction. The next day he fell on his own sword. Saul started out as a man who sought God's leadership, but because of the lust for power, he drew so far away from God that he could no longer reach Him.

How can I improve my relationship with God?

Most Christians feel that if they are going to church regularly, they are abiding in Christ. But truly abiding in Christ is much deeper than just attending church, or even reading the Bible. Abiding in Christ is an act of obedience. If you read through the life of King Saul, you will quickly find that he was rebellious toward God. When God demanded that Saul destroy the living things of the Amalikites, including all the livestock, the people, and even the king, Saul refused to obey. After he had conquered the land, he allowed his troops to loot the city and keep the livestock. He also kept the king alive. When Samuel saw this, he told Saul, "To obey is better than sacrifice…for rebellion is as the sin of witchcraft and stubbornness is as the iniquity of idolatry. Because thou hast rejected the Word of the Lord, he hath also rejected you from being king."

Everyone has been rebellious to God at one time or another. That is the nature of sin. Obedience is the only way we can abide in Him. In chapter five we discussed the New Testament parable about the builders. One built his house on the rock, while the other built his on the sand. The purpose of this parable was to show that the house on the rock was like those who hear the Word of God and obey, while the house on the sand was like those who hear the Word but do not obey.

Truly abiding in the vine has nothing to do with time spent in church, in prayer, or in the Word. It does not matter how many homeless people we serve, or for how many orphans we provide. Abiding in the vine is determined by our obedience to God. If we are obedient, we will bear much fruit, but if we are not obedient, we can do nothing.

Why is there no fruit?

A branch is not fruitful when the life-source has been cut off. This can be due to disease or damage. Think about the nervous system of the body. It is an electrical system that runs through the body, and if something happens that breaks the connection, the system cannot send the proper signals.

The human body constantly regenerates new cells. Bones and muscles can be repaired. Damage or illness can heal over time. However, since nerve tissue is the slowest growing tissue, once the nerve is broken, it naturally will not recover.

In much the same way, when the life-source of the branch is cut off due to sin and a broken relationship, it can be very difficult for a person to reconnect with God. This is what we see in the life of Saul. He knew that his relationship with God was broken, but he wanted so badly to receive a message from God. He broke his own law and met with a medium to conjure up the spirit of Samuel. In 1 Samuel 28, Samuel rebukes Saul for what he had done and then reveals that Saul and his son Jonathan would soon die in battle.

It is very important that we allow God to help us work through problems in our lives before we grow so hardened that we sever our relationship with God. God, in His abundant grace and mercy, gives us time to eliminate the things that tie us down. He gives us the power of life through His Spirit to overcome the sin that tries to keep us bound. If we ever get to the point that we turn our backs on God and sever that relationship, there is a chance that we will never be able to turn back.

When a branch is so far gone that it can no longer flow with life, it is good for nothing. It then has to be cut down and cast into the fire. In the Bible the fire speaks of judgment, and here it refers to the final judgment of the second death.

For this reason, it is dire that we as Christians continue to examine ourselves and be honest. It is so easy for us to overlook fatal flaws. If we continue to look deep within our hearts and pull out the weeds, pruning down the dead brush and purging out any disease, we will be fruitful. Our relationship with God is our responsibility to maintain. Moreover, with God's help we can do all things.

Chapter 24 – Empowered to Shine

In this final chapter we are going to discuss the end-all goal of the Holy Spirit. The reason that God gave us the Holy Spirit was to empower us to advance the Kingdom of God. Regardless of what a person's doctrine or believe system is, most believers would agree that God sent His Spirit into the world to help us in our Christian walk. In everything we do, we are representatives of God's love to a lost and broken world.

As we grow closer in our relationship with God, we are better equipped to demonstrate His love through our actions. People can see the essence of God in the way that we handle problems and situations. Other individuals can recognize the difference that God has made in our lives. And recognizing that fact can promote the desire to invite God into their lives.

How am I salt of the Earth?

In chapter 4 we introduced Jesus' words found in Matthew 5:13, "Ye are the salt of the earth: but if the salt has lost his savor, wherewith shall it be salted? It is thenceforth good for nothing, but to be cast out, and to be trodden under foot of men." When reading this passage many people ask, "How can salt lose its savor?" Salt has been around since the beginning of time. How can a stable compound like salt effectively lose its taste?

Sadly, since we live in the 21st Century, it is difficult for us to determine Jesus' exact meaning; however, the Jews of the time would have understood what Jesus was saying. Salt was very commonplace in the Jewish home. Typically, it was used for many different purposes, not only as a seasoning. Salt's primary use was as a preservative to keep food from spoiling. Unlike the finely processed salt that we think of today, the Jews got a lot of their salt from salt marshes. These marshes were low-lying areas found primarily around the Dead Sea, which, as many know, contains such high salt content that plants and fish cannot survive there. The salt in these marshes could be mixed with any number of other chemicals, some of which may not even be safe for human consumption. This salt compound would not be able to effectively preserve food. The ancient people would take this salt and mix it with the paving for streets and pathways. While this salt was adequate for cutting down on the overgrowth of grass along the pathways, it was no longer suitable to use in food or for preservation.[83]

Instead of "losing its savor" the New American Commentary translates it more literally as "is defiled[84]." when Jesus speaks of salt losing its savor, he is speaking of salt that has been so intermixed with other chemicals that it was no longer suitable to be used for food, either for consumption or for preserving. It would be thrown out into the pathway

---

[83] Radmacher, Earl D., Ronald Barclay Allen, and H. Wayne House. *The Nelson Study Bible: New King James Version.* (Nashville: Nelson Publishers, 1997).

[84] Bloomberg, Craig, Vol. 22, *Matthew*, electronic ed., Logos Library System; The New American Commentary, (Nashville: Broadman & Holman Publishers, 2001), p102.

and be trampled on by passersby. In like manner, when we allow ourselves to be completely integrated into and corrupted by the world, we take on its values and characteristics becoming non-effective as witnesses. When we choose to emulate the lifestyles of the world, we are not valid representatives of Christ.

However, Jesus is also not saying that we need to completely separate ourselves from the world in order to maintain our witness. He says that we shall be in the world, but not of it. Rather, He is speaking of not allowing the world to pollute our Christianity. For a preservative or seasoning to be valuable, it must come in actual contact with the food that it is supposed to be seasoning. Jesus is saying, "You are the preservative of the earth. You are the ones who will preserve Christianity and the Gospel in the world." To be that preservative, we must encounter the world, but not allow our Christianity to be watered down or poisoned by the ways of the world.

Jesus did not separate Himself from the world; instead, Jesus encountered the world every day of his life. He lived with sinners, dined with tax collectors, and spent time with prostitutes. Yet Hebrews tells us, "He sinned not." He did not sin because He did not allow His Spirit to become tainted by the fleshly enticements of the world.

How can I be the light of the World?

In Matthew, chapter 5, starting with verse 14, it says, "Ye are the light of the world. A city that is set on a hill cannot be hid. Neither do men light a candle, and put it under a bushel, but on a candlestick, and it giveth light unto all that are in the house. Let your light so shine before men, that they may see your good works, and glorify your Father which is in heaven." Your light is an example for all people. It is the light that shines in the darkness. John tells us that Jesus was the light of the world. And now since the physical manifestation of Jesus is not present in the world, we are the light that He is shining through. He is active through us.

When we are baptized in the Holy Spirit, we take on a new identity. We take on the Identity of Jesus Christ in the world. He is the Light and shines out through us. The Holy Spirit empowers us to be God's representatives in the world. In Acts 1:8, Jesus said, "But ye shall receive power, after that the Holy Ghost is come upon you: and ye shall be witnesses unto me both in Jerusalem, and in all Judea, and in Samaria, and unto the uttermost part of the earth."

The Greek word for power used here speaks of an empowerment by God. It is the enabling or empowering of the Spirit who works in our lives. We can live in grace because the very same power that Jesus manifested dwells inside of us.

In John 14:16-17, Jesus says that He will pray that God will send another comforter. The word "another" does not refer to something different, but rather something made up of the same essence as Jesus Christ. The Holy Spirit's power is the same essence as Christ Jesus and now lives inside of us just as it was evident in the Lord Jesus. As Jesus is the light unto the world, so are we.

What is the Goal of the Spirit?

We also discover in Act 1:8, that we are given the Holy Spirit to enable us to be effective witnesses for Christ. The empowerment of the

Holy Spirit was not simply so we could perform signs and wonders or prophesy, but so that we could witness to the world.

First Peter, Chapter two, verses 9 & 10 declare, "But ye *are* a chosen generation, a royal priesthood, a holy nation, a peculiar people; that ye should show forth the praises of him who hath called you out of darkness into his marvelous light." We were all lost in the darkness. We were lost in sin, and there was no light in us, but He called us out of the darkness into His marvelous light. Where there is light, there is no darkness.

If we flip the light switch on in a room, the light chases the darkness away. Similarly, when the light of God enters our lives, the darkness must flee, allowing us to represent the light to the world. God chose us to express His power in the world by the manifestation of His Spirit.

For instance, in John chapter 4, Jesus was talking to the Samaritan woman at the well. He spoke a divinely inspired word of knowledge to her. If His abilities were merely human, there's no way He could have known about her past. But because of His divine, omniscient nature, He knew that she had been married multiple times and that the man that she was then living with was not her husband. The same Holy Spirit that dwells inside of you is the Spirit of God that worked through Christ. In John 14:12, Jesus said that we would be empowered to do works on a larger scale than He was able to do while on earth.

Since Jesus' miracles help to spread the Good News, the miracles and healings that God is still producing in the world continue to demonstrate God's love for the world. As we actively walk with Him, we help to share God's message with unbelievers. We demonstrate God's power and it helps to promote the message of salvation.

Where do I shine?

Jesus said, "You will be my witnesses in Jerusalem, all Judea, Samaria, and to the ends of the world." Jerusalem represents your immediate location and the people in it. Just as the Christians in the early church began ministering in the city of Jerusalem first, our first goal is to let the power of Jesus be evident to those immediately surrounding us.

This is possibly the hardest group to reach because they see us all the time. Jesus found it difficult to reach out to His immediate family and even to those in His home town. As we pointed out previously, He even stated, "A prophet is not without honor except in his hometown."[85] The people we are the closest to see our faults and failures. They see everything about us and know everything we have ever done. They have seen us at our highest and have seen us at our lowest. However, they are the first upon whom we need to shine our light.

Next, Jesus says "all of Judea", which speaks of the area outside our immediate vicinity. We can minister to those at work, those whom we encounter daily at the store or the bank, and those with whom we are acquainted. They are the next group to whom we should witness. We do not see them all the time. They make up our lives but are unrelated to us. The fruit that we let grow in us illuminates others through our example of Christ Jesus. The fruit of the Spirit is not just to dwell inside us; it should be evident to everyone that we meet. Daily, we continually plant the seed

---

[85] Mark 6:4

of the Word in the lives of others. The Bible says that others may water the seed, but it is God who brings the increase.[86]

Samaria represents those that we are not accustomed to. They may be of a different religion, a different denomination, or just people that we do not like or agree with. We can love someone with a Godly love even though we do not agree with them.

The Samaritans were a group of people that the Jews abhorred for several reasons. First, following the reign of King Solomon in the Old Testament, the Jewish tribes separated. The Northern ten tribes banded together and continued to worship God at the altar called Bethel that was originally set up by Abraham. Under several different rulers they began worshiping pagan idols as well. The southern two tribes of Judah and Benjamin continued to worship God at the Temple in Jerusalem. In other words, the basic tenants of their religions were different. The Southern Jews disagreed with the Northern Tribes' worship because it originated as a rebellion against the blood line of King David.

Secondly, the capture of the Northern Kingdom by the Assyrians brought in gentiles, or heathens, to replace the Israelites who were taken captive and led out of Israel as an attempt to thwart future uprisings. The Jews that remained intermarried with the heathens. The Jews, those who lived in Judea, disagreed with intermarriage of God's chosen people with those who worshiped other gods; therefore, they felt that the Samaritans, as their progeny came to be known, should not receive the full blessing from God because they were not completely Jewish. The idea of a pure blood line began in the Torah (Jewish Law). God had instructed the

---

[86] 1 Corinthians 3:6-9

Israelites not to intermarry the people of Canaan. So, the Children of Israel living in the Southern Tribes believed that the remaining Northern Jews were in violation of God's law.[87]

    While it is true that we will never fully agree with everyone, we can always let the light of Jesus shine like a beacon to influence the lives of even those with whom we disagree. As we bear the Fruit of the Spirit in our lives, that Fruit can spread seed in their lives as well. Sharing that fruit could be an act as simple as a smile or a helping hand, but God can take that one small act of kindness and use it to change a person's life.

    Finally, we are taking the light to the uttermost parts of the world. Our actions can reach around the globe. Maybe we cannot go on our own, but we can supply a way for others. We can choose to sow a seed in the life of a missionary or a minister, and we could see returns from that seed reaching all the way around the world. Even if we do not see those returns ourselves, I believe God will see those returns and accredit them to our acts of faith. People in places we could only dream about going can experience an awakening in which the Fruit of the Spirit can blossom in their lives from the seed we have planted.

    Living an empowered life means to live life shining out the light of God into a darkened world. There is a world out there of people who need the love of Jesus Christ. We may be the only light that they see. The candle is placed upon the candlestick to give light to everyone in the house just as we have been placed in the lives of people so that we can be the living light unto them.

---

[87] Ibid.

People do not need to see Christians who think they are high and mighty, who are separated from them by an abyss of pride and self-righteousness. They want people with whom they can relate. We can be those Christians. The seed was planted in us so that we can grow and blossom in an ugly world. We are the ones who will make a difference, so it is time to let the Spirit shine through us.

Works Cited

Aland, Barbara, et al. *The Greek New Testament.* 4th ed. Federal Republic of Germany: United Bible Societies, 1993, c1979.

Aurelius, Marcus. *Meditations.* Brooklyn, NY: Sheba Blake Publishing, 2015.

Biblia Sacra Juxta Vulgatam Clementinam. Electronic Ed. Bellingham, WA: Logos Research Systems, Inc., 2005.

Blomberg, Craig. *Matthew - The New American Commentary.* Electronic. Vol. 22. Nashville: Broadman & Holman Publishers, 2001.

Bruce, F. F. *The Epistle to the Galatians: a Commentary on the Greek Text.* Grand Rapids: W.B. Eerdmans, 1982.

Bundy, Ted, interview by James Dobson. *Fatal Addiction: Ted Bundy's final interview* (January 23, 1989).

Cole, R. Dennis. *Numbers.* Electronic Edition. Vol. 3B. Nashville: Broadman and Holman Publishers, 2001, c2000.

Elwell, Walter A, and Barry J. Beitzel. *Baker Encyclopedia of the Bible.* Vol. 2. Baker Book House: Grand Rapids, 1988.

Elwell, Walter A., and Philip Wesley Comfort. *Tyndale Bible Dictionary.* Wheaton, IL: Tyndale House Publishers, 2001.

Work Cited

Friberg, Timothy, Barbara Friberg, and Neva F. Miller. *Analytical Lexicon of the Greek New Testament.* Vol. 4 of Baker's Greek New Testament library. Grand Rapids: Baker Books, 2000.

George, Timothy. *Galatians.* Electronic ed. Logos Bible Software; the New American Commentary. Vol. 30. Nashville: Broadman and Holman Publishers, 2001, c1994.

Green, Michael P., ed. *Illustrations for Biblical Preaching: Over 1500 Sermon Illustrations Arranged by Topic and Indexed Exhaustively.* Grand Rapids: Baker Book House, 1989.

Hamon, Bill. *Seventy Reasons for Speaking in Tongues: Your Own Built in Spiritual Dynamo.* Shippensburg, PA: Destiny Image Publishers, 2012.

Hayford, Jack A, and Herman Rosenberger. "Appointed to Leadership: God's Principles for Spiritual Leaders,." In *Spirit-Filled Life Kingdom Dynamics Study Guides.* Nashville: Thomas Nelson, 1994.

Heiser, Michael S. "Lust." In *New Bible Dictionary*, by D. R. W. Wood, I. H. Marshall, A. R. Millard, J. I. Packer, & D. J. Wiseman. Downers Grove, IL: InterVarsity Press, 1996.

Jeremiah, David. *The Power of Love : Study Guide.* Nashville: Thomas Nelson Publishers, 2004.

Jethani, Skye. "Apostles Today?" *Christianity Today*, Spring 2008.

Keener, Craig S. and InterVarsity Press. *The IVP Bible Background Commentary : New Testament.* Downers Grove,, IL: InterVarsity Press, 1993.

Kelton, David. *Chosen To live.* New Kensington, PA: Whitaker House, 1986.

King James Version Bible. Electronic Edition. Willingham, WA: Logos Research Systems, 1995.

Lewis, C.S. *The Screwtape Letters.* New York: Harper Collins, 1942, 1996.

MacArthur, John. *Galatians.* Chicago: Moody Press, 1996, c1987.

Miller, Carmen. *Remembering Billy Graham: 20 Memorable Quotes.* February 21, 2018. http://www.wholemagazine.org/posts/remembering-billy-graham-20-memorable-quotes (accessed September 22, 2018).

Newberry, Thomas, and George Ricker Berry. *The Interlinear literal Translation of the Greek New Testamnet.* Bellingham, WA: Logos Research Systems, Inc., 2004.

Newman, Barclay Moon, and Philip C. Stine. *A Handbook on the Gospel of Matthew.* New York: UBS helps for translators; UBS handbook series, 1992.

Peterson, Eugene H. *The Message: The Bible in Contemporary Language.* Colorado Springs, CO: NavPress, 2002.

Work Cited

Proven Men Ministies. *2014 Pornography Survey and Statistics.* December 29, 2015. http://www.provenmen.org/2014pornsurvey (accessed Sepember 15, 2018).

Radmacher, Earl D., and et al. *Nelson's New Illustrated Bible Commentary.* Nashville: T. Nelson Publishers, 1999.

Radmacher, Earl D., Ronald Barclay Allen, and H. Wayne House. *The Nelson Study Bible: New King James Version.* Nashville: Nelson Publishers, 1997.

Schelmetic, Tracey E. "Lack of Vacation Leads to Burnout and Loss of Productivity." *Workforce Management Today.* November 18, 2013. http://www.workforcemanagementtoday.com/articles/3606 83-lack-vacation-leads-burnout-lost-productivity.htm (accessed July 17, 2018).

Spence-Jones, H. D. M, ed. *The Pulpit Commentary: 1 Corinthians.* Bellingham, WA: Logos Research Systems, Inc, 2004.

Strong, James. *The Exhaustive Concordance of the Bible : Showing Every Word of the Text of the Common English Version of the Canonical Books, and Every Occurrence of Each Word in Regular Order.* Electronic Edition. Ontario: Woodside Bible Fellowship, 1996.

Tan, Paul Lee. *Encyclopedia of 7700 Illustrations : A Treasury of Illustrations, Anecdotes, Facts and Quotations for Pastors,*

Teachers and Christian Workers. Garland, TX: Bible Communications, 1996, c.1979.

The Amplified Bible, Containing the Amplified old Testament and the Amplified New Testament. La habra, CA: the Lockman Foundation, 1987.

The Holy Bible : Today's New International Version. Grand Rapids, MI: Zondervan, 2005.

Thiselton, Anthony C. *The First Epistle to the Corinthians : A Commentary on the Greek Text.* Electronic. Grand Rapids: W.B. Eerdmans, 2000.

Tozer, A. W. *The Pursuit of God.* Dallas, TX: Gideon House Books, 2017.

Tyndale House Publishers. *Holy Bible : New Living Translation.* 2nd ed. Wheaton, IL: Tyndale House Publishers, 2004.

—. *Holy Bible: New Living Translation.* Carol Stream, IL: Tyndale House Publishers, 2013.

Walters, Kerry. *Merciful Meekness: Becoming a Spiritual Integrated Person.* Mahwah, NJ: Paulist Press, 2004.

Williamson, H.G. M., and Craig A Evans. "Samaritans." In *Dictionary of New Testament Background: A Compendium of Contemporary Biblical Scholorship*, by Craig A Evans, & Stanley E Porter, 1057. Downers Grove, IL: InterVarsity Press, 2000.

Work Cited

Wright, N.T. *What Saint Paul Really Said.* Grand Rapids: Eerdmans Publishing Company, 1997.

Wuest, Kenneth S. "Wuest's Word Studies from the Greek New Testament : For the English Reader." Grand Rapids: Eerdmans, 1997.

www.ingramcontent.com/pod-product-compliance
Lightning Source LLC
Chambersburg PA
CBHW052021070526
44584CB00016B/1854